I0766940

Savage LIES

The Half-Truths,
Distortions and Outright Lies
of a Right-Wing Blowhard

Bill Bowman

Truth to Power Media

truthtopowermedia.com

Bowman, Bill
    Savage Lies: The Half-Truths, Distortions and Outright Lies of a Right-Wing Blowhard/Bill Bowman

ISBN 978-1-84728-541-6

truthtopowermedia.com
Printed in the United States of America.

*To PJ, with whom
all things start and end.*

Contents

Introduction

Right from the get—go, let me state, unequivocally, that I really don't care what opinions Michael "Savage" Weiner holds.

I've heard enough of his radio shows, I've read the three books that comprise his "political trilogy," and I've read his columns.

His ideas and opinions are his, and he has every right to them, as all Americans do to our own ideas.

Most of what fills the three books I've examined – *The Savage Nation, The Enemy Within* and *Liberalism is a Mental Disorder* – are Savage's opinions and his takes on current events or certain issues. Some of those opinions are a little over the top, such as his idea that reporters who are critical of the war in Iraq should be prosecuted as traitors. Others are pretty straight-ahead conservative political views, such as multiple examples of the "evils" of Bill and Hillary Clinton. And in other instances, he just states truisms – liberal Democratic politicians favor a woman's right to choose or universal health care insurance — that I suppose are meant to unite his conservative readership in some sort of indignant fellowship.

And there's a fair amount of ridicule in the books as well, a tactic Savage believes is perfectly legitimate in serious political discourse.

Such as on page 19 of *The Savage Nation*, the first book

of the trilogy, where Savage offers this gem: "To fight only the al-Qaida scum is to miss the terrorist network operating within our own borders. Who are these traitors? Every rotten radical left-winger in this country, that's who."

Savage also spends considerable time on flights of fancy, such as when, on page 34 of *The Savage Nation,* he attacks liberals' stance on multi-culturalism by asserting that they would outlaw the color white.

Do I agree with his views on dissent? Of course not. As Edward R. Murrow said, we should not confuse dissent with disloyalty. But folks like Savage would probably consider Murrow a traitor as well.

So they're his opinions and he's welcome to them. What irritates me, and what was the impetus for this book, is when he lies, distorts or misstates the truth to buttress those opinions.

Why, if you truly believe in what you say, must you lie to support those ideas?

Savage has been able to get away with this for years because very few people have truth-tested what he says. There have been the occasional Web site or blog that petered out after a short while, but nothing consistent. And his listeners and readers basically play Linda Lovelace to his John Holmes, unquestioningly swallowing whole what he gives them.

So who is Michael Savage, and why should you care if he lies?

Well, Savage is not his real last name. He was born Michael

A. Weiner. He adopted the Savage name shortly before starting his radio career. I guess "Weiner Nation" didn't have the same impact.

As Michael Savage, he is the host of a nationally syndicated radio show based in San Francisco, California, "The Savage Nation," that is heard on several hundred radio stations by a weekly audience of millions.

Just how many millions are up for debate. Savage's Web site says between 8 million and 10 million but Savage, when he's feeling particularly chipper, will say that it's probably more like 20 million.

As Savage, he is also the author of four books – three of which, as I have said, are the subjects of this book – which distill his political philosophy. I have heard him refer to the first three books as his legacy.

Why you should care about his lies is simple. While he may not be on everyone's radar, Savage's show does garner high ratings in its major markets. In his books and on his radio show rants, Savage employs a unique blend of hate and misinformation that is clumsy and, at the same time, apparently effective.

He routinely spits out half-truths and misstatements that he parades as facts and which for the most part go unchallenged. As a result, he not only gets to set the agenda, but he also defines the terms of the debate.

Granted, Savage does not have the audience of a Rush Limbaugh or Bill O'Reilly – two commentators he dislikes and regularly ridicules– but he does have a significant core following.

Allowing Savage and Right-wing blowhards like him to continue setting the agenda and defining the terms of the debate without any checks on the veracity of their comments, I believe, is dangerous in the long run. Staying silent in the face of lies not only tacitly endorses those lies, it emboldens their author to spin more and larger untruths.

And, as University of California-Berkeley professor George Lakoff writes in his book, *Whose Freedom? The Battle Over America's Most Important Idea*, "In politics, whoever frames the debate tends to win the debate."

So this is my attempt at truth-testing the major assertions made by one of Right-wing radio's rising stars.

As I will show in the pages that follow, Savage is not simply an author or a radio host, he is a propagandist. Not a particularly good one, but a propagandist, nonetheless.

"Propaganda" is one of those words with many shades. To some, it is evil incarnate, employed by those whose only goal is to convince their audience of the righteousness of their agenda, all the while obfuscating the true intent of that agenda. To others, it's the noble pursuit of subtle persuasion, as benign as a television commercial, the goal of which is to sell a product or pitch an idea.

The term "propaganda" finds its roots in the Catholic Church in the early 1600s, when Pope Gregory XV formed the Sacred Congregation for the Propagation of the Faith, which was responsible for the spread of Catholicism. (There's a pretty thorough history of propaganda at Wikipedia {en.wikipedia.org/wiki/Propaganda}, which I will distill here).

While it may not have been called such, propaganda has been employed in various forms throughout history, usually in a time of war. The pamphleteer Thomas Paine, for example, is considered the greatest propagandist of the American Revolution.

The modern usage of the term has been dated to World War I, when journalist Walter Lipman and psychologist Edward Bernays, a nephew of Sigmund Freud, further refined its techniques.

Propaganda methodologies have been used, modified and perfected in the decades since then, through World War II, the Cold War and to the present day, in the war against terror.

History has seen its share of successful propagandists – I hesitate to use the term "great" – but perhaps none were so famous, or infamous, as Nazi Germany's Joseph Goebbels.

Goebbels exercised absolute control over the news and information that was disseminated by the country's print and broadcast journalists, all of whom had to be registered through Goebbels' Ministry for Public Enlightenment and Propaganda.

Goebbels and the Nazis did not hesitate to use outright lies to further their goals, whether it was to assure the German people of their eventual success, passing down the latest pep talk from Adolf Hitler, or explaining (and justifying) military actions, such as the invasions that began World War II or expanding the war into Russia.

There are a number of techniques propagandists use in their craft: fear-mongering, using imprecise language, dehumanizing their targets and making them scapegoats, sloganeering, and, of course, lying being chief among them.

Those techniques and more are readily apparent in an even superficial reading of the Savage's political trilogy.

Savage is also fond of comparing his enemies to Adolf Hitler and Nazis in general. That's made more interesting because Savage also delights in dehumanizing his targets, often calling them "vermin" or "rats," which was a favorite tactic of Goebbels.

In fact, some of the similarities in the writings and speeches of Savage and Goebbels are striking.

Here's something Goebbels wrote in 1941: "The Jews are a parasitic race that feeds like a foul fungus on the cultures of healthy but ignorant peoples. There is only one effective measure: cut them out." (http://www.calvin.edu/ academic/cas/ gpa/goeb1.htm).

And here's something Savage said on his radio program on July 6, 2006: "Liberalism is, in essence, the HIV virus, and it weakens the defense cells of a nation." (mediamatters.org/ items/200607110002).

Here's another quote from the Goebbels article referenced above: "The Jews are our destruction. They started this war and direct it. They want to destroy the German Reich and our people. This plan must be blocked."

And this from page 19 of *The Savage Nation*: "Liberalism is unraveling the very fabric of this great nation. And the sooner you understand that liberalism is dangerous mental disorder, the sooner you can break free from this insanity that attacks the way you live, how you conduct your business, the way you worship, the choice of SUV you drive, the food you eat, and the very freedoms you enjoy."

Spooky, huh?

A quick Savage bio: As I've noted, Savage was born Michael Weiner in The Bronx, N.Y., the son of an immigrant. His father, who sold antiques in a small storefront, is the subject of many stories Savage relates during his radio shows and in his books.

Savage – or Weiner, actually — went on to earn master's degrees in anthropology and botany and a Ph.D. in nutritional ethnomedicine, which by some accounts was created solely for him, and hasn't been bestowed upon anyone since. Using that education, he eventually wrote 18 books on herbs and herbal medicine, published under his real name.

Weiner made the switch to Savage – apparently in homage to a South Pacific shipwreck survivor — in the early 1990s and landed a job as a fill-in on a local radio station. He was soon given a full-time gig, and went national in 2000 on Talk Radio Network.

Savage defines himself alternatively as a "Compassionate Conservative" — he claims to have coined that phrase around 1994, and alleges that George W. Bush appropriated it for his 2000 presidential run against Al Gore, although the phrase and the philosophy had already been codified in 1992's *The Tragedy of American Compassion* by University of Texas journalism professor Marvin Olasky — and a nationalist, but is probably not a Nationalist, in the sense of belonging to the Learned, Miss.-based Nationalist Movement, run by Richard Barrett.

Savage has achieved no small amount of success in the years he has been a political commentator. His radio program, "The Savage Nation," is now heard on more than 370 stations nation-wide.

He's continually listed in *Talkers* magazine as one of the top 5 conservative radio yappers, and all his books have appeared on the *New York Times* best-seller list.

Savage imported his radio show to the MSNBC cable network for about five months in 2003, until he was unceremoniously canned after telling a caller whom he thought to be gay to "get AIDS and die."

An interesting side note to the MSNBC incident: Savage tries to mount a defense of himself in *The Enemy Within*, in which he said he was viciously attacked by the caller and thought that he had given the "cut" sign to his producer so that no one would hear what he was saying. But, if you review the video and the transcript (which can be found at www.glaad.

org/eye/media_library/michael_savage.php?#), you'll see that Savage never gave any signal before he went into his rant. And the vicious attack?

The crank caller, who makes a habit of calling shows to plug his favorite radio program, suggested that Savage get some dental work done because his teeth were "really bad."

Savage's political philosophy can be summed up in three words: borders, language and culture. He believes the country should promote English as the national language (for example, he's against the printing of election ballots in several languages), close all borders to prevent illegal immigration (and send those who are now here illegally back to their home countries) and protect our "American culture," which includes such core Conservative ideas as abolishing all racial quotas and enacting a Constitutional amendment defining marriage as being between a man and a woman. He also advocates for the deportation of political Liberals and the dissolution of the American Civil Liberties Union and prosecution of its leaders for either sedition (even though the Sedition Act was repealed in 1921) or under the Racketeer Influenced and Corrupt Organizations Act. Savage is convinced that the ACLU receives much of its funding from terrorist organizations.

He continually rails against Liberals, for whom – in the best tradition of Goebbels — he has a number of pet names, such as "Red Diaper Doper Babies," "Lunchroom Lenins," and "Demoncats."

Savage has even less regard for those in the entertainment industry who espouse Liberal or Progressive views: "Stand-up Stalins (comedians)," Yenta-tainers," and "Mushroom boys (screenwriters)."

That's interesting because much of the public relations material posted on the Web site of Rockstar Energy Drink — founded by his son, Russell Goldencloud Weiner, and which shares an address with Savage's Right-wing foundation, the Paul Revere Society – features pictures of stars of stage, screen, music and sports.

It's Savage's proclivity to coin derogatory names for those he dislikes – and to mercilessly ridicule them — to think up catchy phrases that encapsulate his ideas, and his willingness to distort the truth and tell outright lies which qualifies him as one of the rabid Right's more prominent modern propagandists.

Prominent only because of the notoriety he has won through his radio show, not because he's any good at it.

Like Goebbels before him, Savage is not averse to stretching the truth to achieve his goals. Unfortunately for Savage, as I show in this book, he's usually so inept at spinning his version that many of his assertions don't stand even a minimal truth test.

As you will soon see, Savage's books are littered with quotes taken out of context, misquotes, half-truths, weasel words and outright lies. There are a number of cases where footnotes are misidentified and where he shows amazingly sloppy research techniques, especially for one who holds a Ph.D.

And the liberal (no pun intended) mis-use of statistics is readily evident in all three books.

For example, in *Liberalism is a Mental Disorder*, Savage claims that former President Bill Clinton – one of Savage's favorite targets – was rated as "good" by merely 11 percent of an unnamed population. Look a little closer, and you see that a company that does work with the conservative Heritage Foundation conducted the poll. Another poll, conducted earlier that year by ABC News and the Washington Post, showed that about 62 percent of those polled said they approved of the way Clinton handled the presidency.

In *The Savage Nation*, Savage — without attribution – claims that "Eighty-five to 90 percent of Americans want no more immigrants coming into our nation and changing the demographics of this country. This might sound harsh to you, but the takeover of the United States of America by illegal aliens is a monumental problem."

That's classic Savage: present mixed messages and neglect to provide a source so his assertions can be checked.

Whether or not Savage's claim is true, he leaves out a crucial fact: the book was published in 2002, with the terrorist attacks of September 2001 still very fresh in Americans' minds. Any poll on immigration taken in that time frame would have skewed results, based on people's justified fears about another attack by terrorists who entered the country illegally.

In fact, the Worldviews 2002 report (a yearly project of the Chicago Council on Foreign Relations and the German Marshall Fund of the United States) pointed out that a "comparison of CBS/ New York Times and Gallup polls that asked identical questions about immigration shortly before and after the September 11 attacks shows a 10 percentage point increase after the attacks in the proportion of Americans that favor reducing immigration."

Another tried-and-true propagandist strategy that Savage employs is to scare the heck out of the targeted audience. Again, in *Liberalism*, Savage claims that "(T)he Islamofascists are today, right now, plotting a nuclear attack on our country. According to one of the world's foremost terrorism experts, our Islamofascist enemies have the capability to do so. Yossef Bodansky is on record saying Islamic terrorists have a suitcase nuke."

But Savage leaves out the rest of Bodansky's quote: "At the same time, however, the key terrorism sponsoring states urge prudence, fearing U.S. retribution. Right now, there are intense theological deliberations within the Islamist movement about what to do next. We will surely see the outcome of these deliberations."

Savage displays his facility for sloganeering in all of his books, such as his calling liberals the "Dogs of Hate" in *The Enemy Within* and, in another tirade against immigration, declares the country is becoming "America the chamber pot" in

The Savage Nation.

Not everything that Savage writes is untrue. That is another technique of the propagandist: include just enough truth to make what you say plausible. And one may not completely disagree with everything he writes. My point is that he is so willing to lie and distort the truth and so lazy about his primary research, that anything he writes lacks credibility. And because that is so obvious, Savage has failed as a propagandist.

And he's also intellectually lazy. To get material for his books, Savage has mined a number of columns he wrote for the NewsMax.com Web site over the years. This has resulted in three books of at least 200 pages each.

The problem is, Savage covers the same territory in each of the books, writing about the same topics and sometimes not even bothering to make much of a change to the wording.

What that boils down to is: about 85 percent of each book is comprised of Savage's opinions, twisted logic and those "conservative truisms" I mentioned earlier. The remaining 15 percent or so is lies, misstatements and half-truths.

Savage's predilection to "repurpose" his material precluded me from discussing each book individually. Instead, I took Savage's main topics – such as the Clintons, the Supreme Court, and the "Liberal" media – and present some of the more outrageous examples of his mediocre attempt at propaganda.

I have purposely stayed away from his opinions; like I said, he's entitled to them. I have limited myself to his purported statements of fact so as to present as straightforward a response as possible.

I've checked every endnote and, where he states facts with no attribution, I've searched the on the general subject area or a particular quote. Every refutation I've found has been foot-noted.

I have also stayed away from Weiner's fourth book writing as Michael Savage, *The Political Zoo*, which was published while I was researching this book. In it, Savage ridicules 49 public figures, morphing them into "animals" and assigning them mock Latin names.

In flipping through *Political Zoo*, it didn't appear as though there was anything new presented, thus, I've decided to stop at Liberalism is a Mental Disorder.

What follows, then, are the Savage Lies.

Bill Bowman
August, 2006

The ACLU

One of Savage's favorite targets is the ACLU, which he frequently says should be prosecuted under the federal Racketeer Influenced and Corrupt Organizations Act, also known as RICO.

"The ACLU-Gestapo filed a federal lawsuit against a small town in southeastern Louisiana. Why?
These ACLU-RDDB kooks wanted the good citizens of Franklinton to take down a sign that proclaimed: "Jesus is Lord over Franklinton." If the people of Franklinton don't have a problem with it, what business is it of the ACLU? The ACLU has such nerve. It's gone insane, over the edge. Its goons don't belong in America. They don't belong in this country ... But you absolutely have to agree with me that the ACLU, in attacking religion in this country, is a demented, sick, negative force." **The Savage Nation, page 164**

The problem the ACLU had with the signs is that they were displayed on public property and, as such, broached the wall between church and state. The ACLU was not "attacking religion," as Savage asserts, but was upholding the Constitution, which prohibits government from elevating any one religion over others.

> *"While the ACLU storm troopers were on a roll, they threatened to sue the mayor of Inglis, Florida, unless she removed a proclamation banning Satan within town limits."* **The Savage Nation, page 164.**

Actually, the ACLU decided against the suit because it was assured by members of the town commission that the proclamation had no effect because it was not voted upon.

And here's what the proclamation said[1]:

> *" 'We exercise our authority over the devil in Jesus' name. By that authority . . . we command all satanic and demonic forces to cease their activities and depart the town of Inglis. ...'*
> *The mayor ended the proclamation by saying she was taking this action 'in accordance with our Lord and Savior, Jesus Christ.' "*

---

1   "Satan Ban is Jeered, Cheered," by Associated Press writer Mike Schneider. April 16, 2002.

Apparently, the ACLU wasn't alone in its opposition to the "proclamation." Town residents started a recall petition, but decided to hold off on it, and some commissioners spoke against it.

One commissioner even ran against the mayor in the next election, something that had never been done before.

> *"The officials in New York City have been rightly concerned about another attack. What did they do? They put in place a high-tech surveillance system that scrutinizes the faces of all tourists and guests who visit the Statue of Liberty. The face recognition technology compares each picture to a database of known offenders and terrorist suspects at a rate of one million images a second.*
>
> *"Governor George Pataki was forced to defend his move when the ACLU protested! Pataki said, 'People are still coming to New York City, to the Statue of Liberty, from around the country and around the world because they appreciate that this is a secure, safe and free city.' …Why did the ACLU say about this antiterrorism tool? They charged it was an 'insult to the American people.'"* **The Savage Nation, page 166.**

Pataki defending the system from the ACLU scourge makes

for a good story, but it didn't happen. According to the Associated Press story that Savage is apparently quoting, Pataki's quote in the story was meant to explain a previous paragraph which stated that the technology's use may be expanded to other parts of the city. The ACLU quote doesn't occur until later.

And, according to the ACLU's Web page[2] on the issue, there is cause for concern with the technology. A study of its use at Palm Beach International Airport showed that it failed 53 percent of the time, and that it could be easily compromised.

In talking about the "extremists" of the ACLU, Savage writes:

> *"Extremism in any of its varied forms threatens our democracy and should be avoided at all costs."* **Liberalism is a Mental Disorder, page 148.**

This from the man who compares those he disagrees with to Hitler and who once told a caller to his short-lived cable television show – whom he thought was gay – that he should "get AIDS and die" and choke on a sausage.

> *"Or their best efforts to strip God from the Pledge of Allegiance, while jack hammering the cultural*

---

2   "ACLU Blasts Plan to Use Flawed Facial Recognition System at Statue of Liberty and Other NY Landmarks," American Civil Liberties Union, May 24, 2002. http://www.aclu.org/privacy/spying/14819prs20020524.html

stones upon which this nation was built – the Ten Commandments." **Liberalism is a Mental Disorder, page 149.**

Here Savage the propagandist engages in a little historical revisionism. He'd have his readers believe that the pledge, as it was written, included the phrase "under God." But as it was originally written in 1892 by Francis Bellamy – a Socialist! Baptist minister – the pledge did not reference God. That was on purpose.

Bellamy preached such sermons titled "Jesus the Socialist," and believed that religion was best kept in the home and in church. But, he wrote, the "training of citizens in the common knowledge and the common duties of citizenship belongs irrevocably to the State."[3]

The phrase, "under God" wasn't added to the pledge until the 1950s when the Knights of Columbus convinced President Dwight Eisenhower to support it. At the time, the United States was in the early stages of the Cold War with "Godless Communism."

Savage's assertion that the nation was built upon the Ten Commandments is equally as tenuous. The Religious Right's contention that the U.S. is a "Christian" nation is belied by the fact that "God" never appears in the Bill of Rights or the Constitution, and by quotes from some of the founders.

---

3   Gary DeMar, "The Forgotten History of the Pledge of Allegiance," http://americanvision.org/articlearchive/12-17-04.asp

"History I believe furnishes no example of a priest-ridden people maintaining a free civil government. This marks the lowest grade of ignorance, of which their political as well as religious leaders will always avail themselves for their own purpose," wrote Thomas Jefferson. "Rulers who wish to subvert the public liberty may have found an established clergy convenient auxiliaries. A just government, instituted to secure and perpetuate it, needs them not," noted James Madison. Are they just brain-addled liberals, too?

I'm not arguing that the founders were atheists – clearly, history and their writings show that most were not — but what I am saying is that the historical record suggests that even though they had religious or spiritualistic beliefs, they recognized that this country should be run by a civil government and not a theocracy.

Gays and Lesbians

"The unenlightened, provincial, 'progressive' lem-mings leading San Francisco have taken another giant leap backward in deciding to pay for sex change surgery and all the 'counseling' and hor-mone shots for 'Tommys' who want to be 'Bettys' and for 'Barbaras' who really want to be 'Willys.' ... In Sicko-Frisco, such insanity is now encour-aged and is covered by the city's 'health plan.' But changing sex is not cheap. For males changing to females, surgery costs about $37,000. For de-ranged females who wish to become males, the price is $77,000." **The Savage Nation, page 41.**

Once again, Savage omits the facts of the story that might weaken his premise. What he didn't tell us is that the plan does not cover the entire cost of the surgery. The plan comes with a $50,000 lifetime cap and requires the patient to pay 15 per-cent of the cost if the doctor is in the city's network of health care providers and 50 percent of the cost if the doctor is out of network.[4]

Savage also doesn't tell us that unlike "traditional" surgery, the sex-change operation coverage does not kick in until an employee has been on the payroll for at least a year.

Rather than tell the full story, Savage distorts the facts in a cheap attempt to rile his readers, a classic technique of the propagandist.

> *"On April 21, 2003, the Democrat-controlled California Assembly passed AB 196, a bill authorizing fines up to $150,000 against any business owner (including churches, schools and nonprofit organizations like the Boy Scouts) who refuses to employ transgender or cross-dressing applicants."* **Liberalism is a Mental Disorder, page 98.**

Once again, Savage either purposely misrepresents the bill, or he relies on and passes forward faulty information.

AB 196 was not as cut-and-dried as Savage implies. It was actually simply an extension of California's anti-discrimination

---

4   "S.F. Set to Add Sex Change Benefits, CityWould be First to Include Options," *The San Fransisco Chronicle*, Feb. 16, 2001.
http://www.sfgate.com/cgibin/article.cgi?file=/chronicle/
archive/2001/02/16/MN202072.DTL

laws, the same laws that prohibit denying blacks or Hispanics jobs and housing based on race or ethnicity.[5]

The bill does not mandate that business must hire transgender people, it just makes it a crime to discriminate against them.

And contrary to his assertion, the bill exempts non-profits such as churches.

> *"A twenty-seven-year-old male prostitute with 'gender identity issues' attempted to hang himself in his jail cell, but botched the effort resulting in brain damage. He sued the city of Philadelphia for $50 million. On what grounds? His lawyers argued that their client should have been placed in a suicide-watch cell, not a conventional police cell. Rather than expend resources to defend itself, the city decided to settle the lawsuit for $3.5 million."* **Liberalism is a Mental Disorder, pages 106- 107.**

Almost. What Savage neglects to mention is that the male prostitute was known to Philly police and had attempted suicide before. In fact, he was kept in a suicide watch cell the last time he had been arrested. According to the Philadelphia Inquirer article Savage cites, the man's prior paperwork showing that

---

5   Full text of AB 196: http://www.geocities.com/neutralcorner/AB196.html

never made it to the proper station.

And contrary to Savage's assertion that Philadelphia officials decided to not defend themselves, the $3.5 million settlement was reached by the time the man's attorney had finished his closing argument.[6]

---

6 "City abruptly settles suicide prevention suit for $3.5 million; A prostitute, 27, with mental health problems hanged himself in a holding cell in 1999," Joseph A. Slobdozian, *The Philadelphia Inquirer*, Nov. 23, 2004.

Affirmative Action/NAACP

*"If the NAACP had existed in WWII.
Again, imagine, for a minute, what would happen if we had to fight World War II in today's climate of ultratolerance. For starters, the NAACP
would sue the U.S. Government for racism. No
doubt they would go to Japan, the Reverend
Jesse Hijackson leading the pack, to work the
system from the other side."* **The Savage Nation, page 55.**

Well, first of all, the NAACP *was* around in World War II. In fact, it was created in February, 1909 in New York City[7].

During World War I, the organization ensured that blacks would be eligible for military commissions. As a result, 600 blacks were commissioned as officers and 700,000 registered for the draft. And, in World War II, rather than sue the gov-

---

7   http://www.naacp.org/about/history/timeline

ernment for racism, the NAACP won a pledge from President Franklin Roosevelt to order a non-discrimination policy in war related industries and federal employment.

The Clintons

One of Savage's favorite propagandist techniques is to bombard his reader with "facts" presented in such as way as to bolster the appearance of their truth. For example, on pages 59 through 61 of *The Savage Nation*, Savage attacks the Clinton Administration over the attack on the USS Cole on Oct. 12, 2000 in the Port of Aden, Yemen. Seventeen sailors were killed when a small boat laden with explosives floated up next to the guided missile destroyer as it was refueling in the port.

Savage claims that the administration "dropped the ball early in the game," implying that the Cole bombing could have been averted if the administration had been more competent.

To support his assertion, Savage asks a number of questions and presents several quotes, all seemingly designed to show his reader that he has an intimate knowledge of what happened, why it happened, and how it could have been prevented.

He implies that crew members aboard the Cole should have

been able to challenge the small boat as it approached, and asked if there had been a directive from above not to do that.

And why, Savage asks, was there no strong military presence on the destroyer's decks?

> *"Why was deck security lax or nonexistent? Did Madame Halfbright (Savage's derogatory term for Clinton Secretary of State Madeleine Albright) order a 'nonthreatening' deck presence to placate Yemeni sensibilities? Was the crew afraid to act, fearing accusations of /racial profiling' against Arabs?* **The Savage Nation, page 60.**

Savage returns to this theme in the other two books on the trilogy, making basically the same assertions. Clinton-bashing is great sport in Right-wing circles, after all.

But as Admiral Vern Clark said on CNN on Oct. 15, 2000, US Navy ships had been refueling at Yemen for about 18 or 19 months prior to the attack, with no incident[8].

In fact, Clark said in that appearance, the US military had decided that, given Yemen's reputation as a haven for terrorists and the country's stated desire to eradicate that reputation, the military would help in that effort by taking actions such as refueling their ships in its port. And guess who championed that

---

8   CNN Late edition transcript, Oct. 15, 2000: http://transcripts.cnn.com/
     TRANSCRIPTS/0010/15/le.00.html

effort? None other than Gen. Tommy Franks, later to be one of the architects of the Iraq War.

As far as the Cole's crew being able to blast that tiny boat out of the water, Clark later said that that would not have occurred to them. Small boats, he said, were always zipping around the larger destroyers for different reasons. There would have been no reason to suspect this particular boat of any ill intent.

As Clark said, "the captain clearly – the ship thought that the boat that is involved was part of a support group that was going to help that tie-up in that port. And that is part of the risk …"

Clark also noted that terrorist attacks against Naval vessels had been a threat since the mid-1980s.

> *"In the name of pragmatism, these 'Third Way' managers push experiments on embryos. To select traits, you see. When challenged by ethicists who see the stalking horse of the extensive eugenics program and other Nazi medical experiments meant to create an unblemished master Aryan race, the smiling, suited thugs say, 'Our moral responsibility is also to take care of our jobs and well-being.'"* **The Savage Nation, Page 63.**

Savage loves to make analogies with Nazis and Nazi Germany. Doesn't matter what he's talking about, sooner or later he'll throw in a Hitler, or Goebbels, or Mengele. But his use of it in that quote is particularly reprehensible.

The "Third Way" to which he refers is a political strategy attributed to Bill Clinton and credited as being the philosophical base for his administration's policies. Savage lumps Clinton, British Prime Minister Tony Blair, former German Chancellor Gerhard Schroeder and former US Senator Tom Daschle under the umbrella of "Third Way managers." And what do they have in common, according to Savage? Of course, they're all socialists.

Savage's reference to "experiments on embryos" has to do with the Clinton administration's support of embryonic stem cell research. Stem cells are the building blocks from which human tissue and organs develop. Stem cell research is controversial because, as anti-abortion groups contend, they are taken from embryos that have not reached full-term and which are destroyed.

Supporters of the research point out that stem cell research could lead to treatments for ailments such as Parkinson's or Alzheimer's disease, or could help repair a damaged heart.

In 1999, the Clinton administration announced that the government would finance research on so-called master cells taken from embryos that the National Institutes of Health had determined were not fetuses. The caveat was that researchers could not use the government money to grow the cells themselves.[9]

---

9   CNN.com Interactive: U.S. government to fund controversial stem cell research. Jan. 19, 1999. http://www.cnn.com/HEALTH/9901/19/stem.cell.research

Stem cell research has nothing to do with "selecting traits," as Savage asserts. Being an educated man, Savage very well knows that (or should) and makes the connection to Nazi medical experiments as a cheap way to agitate. Modern propagandists know that two ways to get people going is to bring up race or the Holocaust.

In a section entitled "Homeland Defense Fund" in *The Savage Nation*, Savage recounts a story that appeared in the Oct. 5, 2001 edition of the *Chicago Tribune* (although he did not specify the date) which talked about lax security at 10 weapons research laboratories in the United States. Army and Navy commando teams, playing the roles of terrorists, were able to break into the labs and, in some cases, get away with large amounts of nuclear material that could have been converted into weapons.

> *"Thank you, former Energy Department Secretary Bill Richardson, who gave us the disappearing hard drives and, of course, the porous fences at our nuclear weapons research and production facilities."* **The Savage Nation, page 64.**

Savage is vastly stretching the point here in yet another attempt to bash the Clinton administration. First of all, Richardson wasn't even named energy secretary until late in 1998.

Blaming him for the "porous fences" at these weapons research labs, that had been around long before he took his post, is just ridiculous.

As for the hard drive comment, Richardson took heat in June of 2000 for two hard drives at the Los Alamos lab that had gone missing for about 11 days. The hard drives – which held information on how to defuse a nuclear weapon — were found in another area of the lab, and the FBI later determined that none of the data had been tampered with.

Savage attempts to blame Richardson for this, but the blame is misguided. Ironically, the Clinton administration had for years tried to upgrade security for sensitive data, but the plans were scuttled after critics – some of whom were legislators who later criticized Richardson for the hard drive incident — said it would limit access to the data.[10]

According to Steve Aftergood of the Federation of American Scientists, if the administration's plans had been accepted, the hard drives

> *"would have been bumped up to the top secret level. And if it had been top secret, then it would have been accountable. And that means it would have been inventoried, it would have been tracked at every moment."*

And, finally, these drills were conducted in 2001, when George W. Bush had assumed the presidency. But Savage, a huge Bush supporter, forgets to mention that.

---

10   Federation of American Scientists News: http://www.fas.org/sgp/news/2000/06/npr061900.html

The *USS Cole* passages in Savage's books underscore more instances where he tried to foist blame on someone who doesn't deserve it:

> *"Why was their dinghy allowed to approach the Cole when the ship was operating under 'Threat Condition Bravo' – the second highest of four security warnings? Why were the sentries on deck required to bear unloaded weapons? Why did the destroyer's rules of engagement require permission from the Cole's captain or another officer before firing?*
>
> *"I'll tell you why: Admiral Vern Clark, chief of naval operations for the Navy under Bill Clinton, said you can't have weapons that fire. The Pentagon-approved rules of engagement for the destroyer basically said you shouldn't show any hostiiility (sic), especially not to our Arab brethren."* **Liberalism is a Mental Disorder, page 13.**

Contrary to Savage's claim, those rules of engagement did not apply solely to the Cole. And there is nothing in the rules that favor Arabs. And as far as not firing on the boat, as Clark explained in an interview, homeports regularly supply "helper boats" to the navy's ships. This boat was seen as one of those boats.

As Clark explained: "All over the world this kind of activity takes place; boats come out and help you; they're part of the thing that supports the harbor there, and when we come to the port, the captain calls in and gets permission to clear the harbor and that's the way that occurs. This boat was part of that evolution.

"They had no reason to suspect, as it has been passed to me, that there was anything to be suspicious about, and then they pulled alongside, and the explosion occurred."[11]

> *"...Bill Clinton was the first president to establish a legal defense fund, the first leader of the free world to be accused of a sexual assault at the White House, the first president sued for sexual harassment, or that the Clinton administration had the largest number of cabinet officials to come under criminal investigation in our history."* **Liberalism is a Mental Disorder, page 136.**

Look, anybody can make charges against anyone. That doesn't make the charges true. But thanks to the climate of today's media – including the Internet – just an allegation is enough to cause fits in a politician's PR office or ruin a life.

Richard Nixon didn't need a legal defense fund, he resigned in disgrace before he could be impeached in the Watergate epi-

---

11   News Hour with Jim Lehrer, http://www.pbs.org/newshour/bb/ military/july-dec00/cole_10-13.html

sode. And enough of Ronald Reagan's underlings fell on their swords for The Gipper that a legal defense fund wasn't necessary in the Iran/Contra scandal.

Thanks to some really zealous prosecution by Republican hacks, Clinton was forced to establish a fund. So what? The man was accused and needed to defend himself, which he did.

Savage attempts to imply in the last accusation that Clinton's administration was the most corrupt in American history.

Again, anyone can be accused of anything. But let's look at the facts: While there may have been many investigations of the Clinton administration, the truth is there were no convictions. Contrast that with the Reagan years, during which 32 members of his administration were convicted, although three of those convictions were overturned, and another 30 appointees resigned or were fired for ethical violations. And let's not even talk about Nixon's administration.

> *"A mere 11 percent claimed Bill was a 'good' president."* **Liberalism is a Mental Disorder, page 138.**

Savage cites a poll conducted by The Polling Company of Washington, D.C., whose clients include the conservative Heritage Foundation. The write-up of the poll appeared in the Nov. 26, 2004 edition of NewsMax.com.

As usual, Savage relies on one source to make his point. But the funny thing about poll numbers is, you can usually find one to dispute another. For example, in an ABC News-Washington Post poll conducted from June 17-20, 2004, 62 percent of those polled said they approved of the way Clinton handled the presidency.[12]

> *"Another extreme measure under consideration by the unhappy political strategists on the left is to rescind the Twenty-second Amendment so that Bill Clinton can run for a third term. Clinton, in true narcissistic flair, floated this absurd notion saying, 'I think since people are living much longer ... the 22nd Amendment should probably be modified to say two consecutive terms instead of two terms for a lifetime.' Really! How would that serve the country?"* **Liberalism is a Mental Disorder, page 193.**

In his zeal to once again bash the former president, Savage must have missed the modern history of the movement to repeal the 22nd Amendment, which limits presidents to two, four-year terms.

No less than Ronald Reagan posited the idea of repealing the amendment in 1986. Frustrated after his reelection by

---

12 Bill Clinton: Job Rating, Pollingreport.com: http://www.pollingreport. com/clinton-.htm

people focusing on the 1988 election rather than on the business at hand, Reagan came to regard presidential term limits as a mistake.

As reported by the *Washington Post*, "Echoing the arguments of the Democrats who tried in 1947 to prevent a unanimous Republican majority from passing their vengeful amendment, Reagan said, 'Shouldn't the people have the right to vote for someone as many times as they want to vote for him?

'They send senators up there for 30 or 40 years, congressmen the same.' "[13]

In Clinton's case, he also said that he knew the rescission would not apply to him. But you won't hear that from Savage.

---

13   Lou Canon, "Short-Sighted Amendment," *The Washington Post*, June 16, 1986.

Liberals and the Environment

Writing about comments on the environment and global warming that a Democrat operative made after the 2004 election, Savage opines:

> "To cite an example of why this nut job believed
> the environment was such a hot topic for the
> Democrats to latch on to, he said, 'I believe global
> warming is more important than we thought.
> Because I've lived through two recent hurricanes
> in Florida, I've come to understand the dangers
> of global warming.'
> "I had to put down my remote control because
> I was laughing so hard. I could not believe this
> man suggested a connection between the hur-
> ricanes in Florida and SUVs!" **Liberalism is a
> Mental Disorder, page XXII.**

First, Savage makes the snide comment about SUVs with no knowledge of what the operative's beliefs on global warming are, although Savage makes clear his views on the topic.

To get to the facts, I need go no further than the National Oceanic and Atmospheric Administration's Geophysical Fluid Dynamics Laboratory. Scientists there have predicted that "The strongest hurricanes in the present climate may be upstaged by even more intense hurricanes over the next century as the earth's climate is warmed by increasing levels of greenhouse gases in the atmosphere."[14]

And then there's this, from the same Web site: "An implication of these studies is that if the frequency of tropical cyclones remains the same over the coming century, a greenhouse-gas induced warming may lead to an increasing risk in the occurrence of highly destructive category-5 storms."[15]

Then there's this from the U.S. Environmental Protection Agency: "Confirmation of 20th-century global warming is further substantiated by melting glaciers, decreased snow cover in the northern hemisphere and even warming below ground."[16]

Finally, the EPA Web site quotes from a 2001 report by the Intergovernmental Panel on Climate Change: "There is new and stronger evidence that most of the warming observed over the last 50 years is attributable to human activities."[17]

---

14 GFDL/NOAA "Global Warming and Hurricanes, http://www.gfdl.noaa.gov/~tk/glob_warm_hurr.html.
15 GFDL/NOAA, "Global Warming and Hurricanes."
16 U.S. EPA Web site on global warming: http://yosemite.epa.gov/oar/ globalwarming.nsf/content/climateuncertainties.html.
17 U.S. EPA Web site on global warming.

Politics

> *"The streets are crawling with crazy people with guns in their hands. The gun grabbers should take the guns away from the psychopaths. But instead, the Diane Feinsteins of the world, the Charlie Schumers, the subway senators, they want to take the guns away from the middle class, leaving us completely defenseless while they remain protected by the Secret Service."*
> **The Savage Nation, page 14**

Savage belly flops into the propagandist's bag of tricks by engaging in a bit of hyperbole, then just blatantly lying.

The streets are crawling with crazy people with guns? Please.

And as far as U.S. Senators being given Secret Service protection, that's just not true.

The Secret Service protects sitting presidents and vice

presidents, those next in succession, their immediate families, former presidents and their families (on a limited basis), visiting heads of state and major presidential and vice presidential candidates.[18]

Senators are not included in that list, a point Savage chooses to ignore.

> *"To fight only the al-Qaida scum is to miss the terrorist network operating within our own borders. Who are these traitors? Every rotten, radical leftwinger in this country, that's who. For years, these empty skirts have been waging a personal war against the American people. They smile for the camera as they spew their phony message of tolerance, diversity and perversity."*
> **The Savage Nation, page 19.**

This isn't exactly a hard fact, but I wanted to include it as an example of Savage's penchant for demonizing those he considers his enemy, in this case, those on the Left. Actually, dehumanizing the enemy is a classic propagandist technique, as is smearing the enemy with allegations that could be true, but can't easily be proven or disproved. Savage is pretty good at spewing wild accusations with no facts to back them up. But

---

18 United States Secret Service Protective Mission:
    http://www.secretservice.gov/protection.shtml

then, when you're preaching to the converted, facts just get in the way.

The Savage Nation in particular is filled with these types of allegations and sweeping generalizations – in fact, the 30 or so pages following this quote are replete with them. They're easy to write, but hard to prove. And, because there are no footnotes provided, the casual reader won't bother to try to check them out. How convenient.

On pages 31 to 33 of *The Savage Nation*, Savage purports to tell the story of Richard Oulton, a decorated Vietnam Vet who ran afoul of his homeowner's association in Richmond, Va. Oulton received two violation notices from his association after he raised an American flag and Purple Heart flag – on separate flag poles – in front of his home.

As Savage tells it, the association fined and later took Oulton to court simply because he wanted to fly the flags. After several years of litigation, Oulton was ordered to pay more than $158,000 to the association, as well as remove the flags and their poles.

At the end of the story, Savage huffs, "This public servant had to drain his retirement savings in order to fight for his right to fly a flag."

Of course, the case wasn't as cut-and-dried as Savage would have us believe.

Like all other common-ownership associations, Oulton's

development, Wyndham, has a set of bylaws by which all home-owners must abide. Included in those bylaws was a prohibition against installing flagpoles in front of homeowners' properties.

That land is called common area and is technically owned by all the homeowners in a development.

Oulton, right or wrong, violated *that* prohibition. He said the flag he wanted to fly was "too small" for the pole on his house, which *had* been approved by the association board.[19]

So Oulton installed the two flag poles – one 16 feet and one 20 feet – and hoisted his flags.

The judge had no choice but to agree with the association and order Oulton to remove the flag poles.

It's important to note that the association did not ban the flying of flags, just the installation of flag poles – or any other structure – on the property. But Savage conveniently leaves that part out and instead chooses to wrap himself in the flag and obfuscate the issue in a patriotic haze of distortion and self-righteous pronouncements.

> *"In South Africa, as a result of the she-ocracy and*
> *the hate crimes laws, it is now a bad thing, yes, a*
> *hate crime, to say that someone is obese. It is also*
> *a crime to say such felonious things as someone*
> *is elderly, married, youthful, disabled, aged or*

---

19 "Wyndham Sues Over Flagpoles; Covenants At Issue, Foundation Asserts," *The Richmond Times Dispatch*, Dec. 22, 1999.

gay. These are the new 'four-letter' words in South Africa." **The Savage Nation, page 38.**

Savage really stretches the truth here. The South African government in 2000 passed the "Promotion of Equality and Prevention of Unfair Discrimination Act," which defines hate crimes and establishes "equality courts" to adjudicate charges of bias and discrimination.

The act establishes three grounds on which one cannot discriminate or communicate hate speech: race, gender or disability.[20]

In terms of hate speech, the act prohibits any communication which could be found to demonstrate a "clear intention to be hurtful, be harmful or incite harm, or promote or propagate hatred."

Remember, this only applies to the three "grounds" I mentioned above. So calling someone youthful, or married, or elderly certainly would not be a violation of the law, no matter how Savage tries to spin it.

"If we had the hiring and the affirmative action rules that are in place today; if we had the radical mad-dog feminists who run so many elements in the federal government today; if the

---

20   The Promotion of Equality and Prevention of Unfair Discrimination Act; http://www.parliament.gov.za/pls/portal/web_app.utl_output_doc?p_table=acts&p_doc_col=act_doc&p_mime_col=mime_type&p_id=50977

*Red Diaper Doper Baby psychopaths from NYU,
Columbia, and Princeton Law that are in place
today were around in 1940, I can tell you without
a shadow of a doubt, this country would have
lost World War II. And I can prove it to you with
one statement. The Manhattan Project."* **The
Savage Nation, pages 55-56.**

Savage goes on to argue that current affirmative action regulations would have forced the government to focus more on ethnicity and gender rather than qualifications in choosing scientists for the Manhattan Project, which search would have led to delays and the eventual destruction of the United States.

Savage's assertions are so ludicrous they almost defy a response.

His charge that the Equal Employment Opportunity Commission would attempt to shut down the project is simply another example of hyperbole used to further a point, regardless of the validity of the underlying assertion.

Savage combines that with some more shoddy research. His reference to "Princeton Law" exemplifies the fact that he writes from the top of his head without the burdens of thought: Princeton has not had a law school since the 1850s.[21]

"Look at the consequences of 'no-fault' divorce

---

21 "A Princeton Companion": http://etcweb1.princeton.edu/
CampusWWW/Companion/law_school.html

and the fallout on the family from these failed liberal doctrines." **The Savage Nation, page 95.**

When it was first enacted in 1969, no-fault divorce was seen as the cure to a broken system of granting divorces that critics said no longer worked. Advocates for change argued that the then-current fault-based system often forced the parties involved to commit perjury, with one staging an adulterous affair to meet the requirements for divorce. Fault-based divorce was also much more contentious, as it allowed the "innocent party" – usually the wife – to receive higher alimony payments and a greater share of marital property.

In 1966, then-California Gov. Edmond G. Brown created the Governor's Commission on the Family and charged it with "the task of addressing ways the family law system, substantively and procedurally, could function more effectively."[22]

The most substantive recommendation developed by the commission was the idea of no-fault divorce. No-fault divorce dictated that there would be no "guilty party" and that all assets would be divided evenly, among other things. The new divorce law was codified in the California Family Law Act of 1969.

Now Brown was a Democrat, and he did get the ball rolling. But the Act was signed into law by none other than ... Ronald Reagan! Certainly no one could confuse Gov. Reagan with a lib-

---

22 "Divorce Reform in California: From fault to no-fault...and back again?" report presented to the California State Assembly Committee on the Judiciary, Nov. 6, 1997. http://www.library.ca.gov/crb/98/04/ currentstate.pdf

eral, especially not in the late 1960s. So Savage once again falls prey to sloppy research or just plain old intellectual laziness in trying to make a point.

Also, notice how Savage rolls no-fault divorce and "failed liberal doctrines" into one big ball, without ever defining what liberal doctrines he's talking about? Savage attempts to support his argument by throwing out statistics concerning "households headed by unmarried persons." The problem with that argument is, of course, the label "unmarried persons" could mean several things, including couples living together who are not married and single parents made single by something other than divorce.

Savage finishes this part of his diatribe by asserting that the "divorce rate has doubled since 1970." He provides no citation for that statement (or any of the others, for that matter), nor could he. Not all states report their divorce rates (including California) and some statistics are based on surveys rather than statistics.

> *"The current congressional redistricting effort is nothing more than political gerrymandering of racial quotas in specific districts to secure a Democratic majority in Congress. Our country is nothing more than a vast checkerboard to these Demoncats, whose only goal is victory at any cost."* **The Savage Nation, page 131.**

Savage scores a rare two-for-one here. He gets to bash Democrats and play the race card at the same time.

What he either doesn't know or conveniently omits is that the redistricting process – usually carried out after each census – is conducted at the state level. So, Democrats would only control it in those states – which don't have bipartisan commissions doing the reapportionment – where they are the majority in the state legislature.

Savage also neglects to mention the most infamous of the redistricting scandals, the one in Texas, perpetuated by Texas Republicans, that eventually led to the legal trouble experienced by former U.S. Rep. Ton DeLay and some of his friends. The new map DeLay helped draw put five veteran Democrat leaders in new districts that slanted heavily Republican.[23]

> *"In America we have lost that which your ancestors died for – our sacred right to vote."* **The Savage Nation, page 187.**

Pretty words. Too bad they're not completely true.

I'm not talking about his claim that we have lost our "sacred right to vote;" that, of course, is ludicrous. I'm talking about his assertion that voting is "our right."

A state can enact legislation to limit the "right" of its citizens to vote at any time. In the early days of the Republic, only

---

23 "Texas Dems face tough odds in new districts," *USA Today,* Oct. 18, 2004

white males of a certain religion were allowed to vote. It wasn't until 1920 that women were allowed to vote. And, as Floridians discovered in 2000, felons are stripped of their "right" to vote in certain states.

For an interesting discussion of the franchise, go to http://www.answers.com/topic/suffrage

In short, most rights are inalienable; privileges are subject to the whim of governors.

> *"A Republican bill introduced into the Senate would have required a photo ID for anyone who wants to vote. We know that photo IDs can be faked, but we know that it is much better than just a signature. Still, there are at least two public enemies with regard to reforming election fraud ... none other than "Upchuck" Schumer in New York ... On the West Coast, it's Ron Wyden of Oregon who wants to block fixing the voting system."* **The Savage Nation, page 187.**

S. 565, the "Martin Luther King Jr. Equal Protection of Voting Rights Act," introduced by Democratic Sen. Christopher Dodd of Connecticut, did indeed carry an amended provision that would require photo identification to vote; but it was for first-time voters who registered by mail. Hardly the voter fraud fixer Savage alleges.

Schumer and Wyden argued that the provision would have

disenfranchised thousands of poor and minority voters who do not have photo IDs. Justified or not, their Senate colleagues agreed because they approved an amendment that substituted a signature for the photo ID.

And the bill eventually passed, 99-1. So much for Savage's claim that the Democrats are prohibiting any "real voting reform".

> *"The jewels of our nuclear secrets were sold to*
> *China for donations to the Gore campaign and*
> *the Democratic National Committee."*
> **The Savage Nation, page 193.**

Savage really outdoes himself with that one. The would-be political analyst tries to take two separate incidents and draw some kind of connection between them. But, as usual, his effort falls far short of the mark.

In writing about the "jewels of our nuclear secrets" being sold to China, Savage is referring to the case of Wen Ho Lee, a Chinese former scientist at Los Alamos National Laboratory in New Mexico. Lee was arrested in 1999 and charged with stealing nuclear secrets for the Chinese.

By 2000, Lee had been pretty much exonerated, with the federal government formally apologizing to him. He currently has a defamation case ongoing.

As far as the donations claim goes, Savage is referring to Johnny Chung, a Chinese-American businessman with ties to the Chinese government. Chung pleaded guilty in 1998 to election law violations and cooperated with Congressional investigators in an examination of practices during Bill Clinton's 1996 presidential reelection campaign.

Of the more than $2 million that Chung received through his business relationships with China, he later testified to a Congressional committee, about 20 percent of that went to political causes. Most went into his own pocket.

And as far as accusations that $300,000 that a Chinese intelligence officer gave Chung to donate to Clinton, federal investigators said only about $20,000 went to the campaign. Chung testified that he kept the rest.[24]

Savage also doesn't pay attention to dates. Al Gore didn't start running for president until 2000. The Johnny Chung affair happened in 1996. But then, Savage was trying to tie alleged improprieties to Gore because he originally wrote this column/chapter in September 2000, the year Gore ran for office.

(For an interesting retrospective on the Chen Ho Lee affair, see the Newshour with Jim Lehrer transcript at http://www.pbs.org/newshour/bb/media/july-dec00/times_9-26.html)

Savage on page 200 of *The Savage Nation* lists "(Al) Gore's 10 Crimes," which he lifted from an Oct. 30, 2000 column he wrote for Newsmax.com. I'll take the "crimes" one at a time:

1. Chinese military operatives stole, bought or were openly

---

24 "Chung tells his fund-raising story to Congress," CNN, May 11, 1999. http://www.cnn.com/ALLPOLITICS/stories/1999/05/11/chung/

given the jewels of our nuclear secrets.

Savage just doesn't want to let that horse die before he gives it a few more kicks. This topic has already been dealt with, but suffice it to say that Gore, as vice president, really had no responsibility for goings-on at the lab at Los Alamos, the alleged theft site.

2. Illegal immigrants from the Middle East, Mexico, China, Africa and Central America broke through our borders.

Interesting, isn't it, how Savage doesn't mention any illegal immigrants from, say, Slavic countries? How he focuses on people of color? I'm just sayin' ...

At any rate, illegal immigration was a problem long before Gore took the Oath of Office and will be a problem for decades to come. In fact, Savage currently rails against George W. Bush for his handling of the illegal immigrant situation. But to present it as a new phenomenon that occurred while Gore was vice president is simply a lie.

3. Homosexual radicals were allowed to attack America's children – e.g., the Boy Scouts.

You'd think by reading this that hordes of lavender-wearing hoodlums were staging raids on Boy Scout camps around the country. What Savage was probably referring to was a suit brought by New Jersey resident James Dale, an Eagle Scout, against the Boy Scouts in 1990 when he was kicked out of the organization because he is gay. The case made it to the New Jersey Supreme Court, which ruled that the Boy Scouts was a "public accommodation" and must allow gays. The Boy Scouts appealed to the U.S. Supreme Court, which reversed the New Jersey ruling and determined that the Scouts is not a public accommodation.

But Savage's message is that Gore, somehow, should have intervened in the case two years before he was in office. Beyond that, Americans have the right to challenge in the courts anything we feel is wrong or unfair. For Savage, the self-proclaimed uber-patriot, to assert anything else is, well, unpatriotic.

4. Leftist radicals were permitted to falsely accuse our police.

Of...what? Brutality? Body odor? Savage just loves to throw out unsubstantiated and, in cases like this, vague assertions and let his readers connect their own dots. Again, anyone can make a claim against anyone else, that's a hallmark of a free society.

But implying that we don't have the right to question a group of people based on their occupation is just laughable.

5. Islam-O-Fascists entered our country through a defacto (sic) open border policy.

Once again, Savage tries to indict Gore for "crimes" committed before his time, and over which he had limited control. Always have been illegal immigrants, always will be.

6. The ACLU was permitted to steal the votes of six million Californians who voted to eliminate free medication and free education to illegal immigrants.

Savage doesn't seem to get the idea of the right of the people to seek redress through the courts, even though he exercised that right when he sued a university for denying him a job interview and filed suits, later dropped, against the owners of two Web sites that criticized him.

In terms of this "crime," the ACLU challenged California's Proposition 187, which would have denied most publicly funded health care to illegal immigrants. The group claimed that the proposition, approved by a popular vote in 1994, was unconstitutional.

A federal judge agreed and, in 1998, struck it down, ruling that the proposition sought to regulate immigration, which only the federal government can do.[25]

And the notion that a successful court challenge to the law could be construed as "stealing" votes is ludicrous.

7. The ACLU was encouraged to drive Christianity out of churches, prayer off playing fields, babies out of wombs, and pornography into every home.

Apparently, Savage would rather Americans get their pornography the way he does, by frequenting peep shows (see the chapter on Sex). But I digress.

This sounds more like one of Savage's radio rants, where he builds on his fulmination until you can practically hear him spitting into the mic. This is just so much hyperbole, aimed at getting his readers fired up and voting against Gore in the 2000

---

25   "Prop. 187 Struck Down: Activists, clinics relieved, but Wilson isn't giving up," by Bert Eljera, *Asian Week*, April 1, 1998.

election.

8. Babies near birth were slaughtered, their body parts sold for profit.

Once again, Savage indulges himself with a sensational statement, minus any attribution or context. Is he talking about late-term abortion? Who knows. But Al Gore, in an Oct. 3, 2000 debate against George W. Bush in Boston, Mass., said that he "would sign a law banning that procedure, provided that doctors have the ability to save a women's life or to act if her health is severely at risk." Gore later said that he supported a woman's right to choose, and charged that Bush "trusts the government to order a woman to do what he (Bush) thinks she ought to do. I trust women to make the decisions that affect their lives, their destinies and their bodies."[26]

9. Innocent Serbian children were bombed and killed.

Innocent Iraqi children were bombed and killed as well, but Savage is not beating his breast over them. Regardless of whether one feels the Serbian bombing campaign was justified, Savage's attempt to pin that decision on Gore, when it was President Clinton's decision, is another example of Savage's love affair with misinformation.

10. The Fourth Amendment was thrown out so little Elian Gonzalez's door could be kicked in without due process.

What? Michael Savage arguing on behalf of an illegal immi-

---

26 Transcript, Boston Presidential debate, *Washington Post.*
    http://www.washingtonpost.com/wp-srv/onpolitics/elections/
    debatetext100300.htm

grant?

Has the sky turned chartreuse?

Elian Gonzalez was the 5-year-old Cuban boy who washed up on the shores of Florida on Thanksgiving Day, 1999 on an inner tube. Elian's mother, step-father and nine others who were trying to escape Cuba, died in the trip.

Elian was taken in by distant relatives, but that custody was challenged by his father in Cuba, who said he wanted his son back. The population of rabid anti-Castroites in the Miami area quickly descended on Elian's case, trying to get him asylum in the U.S.

The case's denouement began with a highly publicized raid on Elian's relatives home, culminating with the famous picture of a terrified Elian being taken out of a closet with an assault rifle inches from his face.

The Clinton Administration decided that Elian's father had the right to bring him back, a decision finally carried out seven months after the boy first washed ashore. This gave Clinton haters yet another reason to foment their anger, but it was Clinton's decision, not Gore's. To attribute this to the vice president is simply pandering.

Besides, as Savage neglects to note, Gore broke with the Clinton Administration on this one and supported efforts to grant Gonzalez and his family permanent legal residence in the United States.

And Savage still isn't done with Elian.

> *"Did you know that all of the other survivors*
> *were granted asylum in America; yet this little*
> *boy was given the bum's rush by the Demoncats."*
> **The Savage Nation, page 201.**

The other two survivors were adults, and had the right to stay. Elian was five at the time, and his father, who had custodial rights, wanted him back in Cuba.

> *"The United States Constitution – especially the*
> *Fourth Amendment – was clearly violated in the*
> *illegal INS Border Patrol machine-gun raid in*
> *the Gonzalez home in Miami."* **The Savage Nation, page 201.**

The Fourth Amendment guarantees citizens protection against unreasonable searches and seizures and requires probable cause for search warrants and the like. In April 2000, federal agents burst into the home of Elian's great-uncle to claim the little boy and return him to his father. U.S. Attorney General Janet Reno said at the time that the government had tried to negotiate with the Gonzalez family, but "the relatives 'kept moving the goal post and raising the hurdles.'

'The Miami relatives rejected our efforts, leaving us no other option but the enforcement option,' Reno said."[27]

---

27 "Elian taken from Miami, reunited with father," Online Newshour Update, April 22, 2000. http://www.pbs.org/newshour/updates/april00/elian_4-22.html

In fact, the Border Patrol agents and U.S. Marshals did have a valid warrant when they raided the Gonzalez home. The U.S. District Court for the Southern District of Florida ruled in June 2001 that the warrant was valid in dismissing some of the counts of a court action brought against Reno and others.[28]

> *"The facts are unmistakable. Certain companies are throwing secret amounts of money to Linda Daschle to line her pocketbook, violating all tenets of decency. She's declined to disclose the identity of the companies or the amounts they've paid for her 'services' as a lobbyist."* **The Savage Nation, page 203.**

Plain and simple, that's just crap.

Federal-level lobbyists have been required to disclose for whom they're working for years. In fact, it took me about five minutes on the Web to find a current list of Linda Daschle's clients, available though a search engine at the U.S. Senate's Office of Public Records (sopr.senate.gov). Had Savage taken the time to look, he (presumably) would have found them, too.

And while I'm in this section, a couple things need to be pointed out. Throughout *The Savage Nation*, Savage does not attribute any of the information he presents as facts. But once

---

28 U.S Court of Appeals, 11th District, March 25, 2003.
    http://caselaw.lp.findlaw.com/data2/circs/11th/0114475p.pdf

in a while, you luck into where Savage gets his information.

For example, on page 202, Savage writes, "Each of the industries Linda represents also has a steady stream of issues before Congress for consideration, and guess who holds the power to set the Senate's agenda? Old dashing Daschle."

Now check out this snippet from a story in the June 5, 2001 issue of USA Today: "The South Dakota Democrat's wife, Linda, is a lobbyist who mostly represents airlines, aircraft makers and other aviation-related interests — all of which have a steady stream of issues before the Senate. As majority leader, Tom Daschle has the power to set the Senate's agenda."

Sounds a *little* similar.

What about this: Savage writes that "Linda Daschle says she will deal with that potential pitfall by never lobbying her husband or any member or committee of the Senate. She says she feels very 'comfortable' with her activities."

Compare that to the USA Today article: "Linda Daschle says she will deal with that potential pitfall the way she has since she resumed her lobbying career in 1997: by never lobbying her husband or any member or committee of the Senate.

'With dual careers in public policy, you need to be careful and take steps to avoid any appearance problem,' she says. 'I feel very comfortable with my activities.'"[29]

---

29 "Daschle, lobbyist wife vow to keep careers separate," by Jim Drinkard, *USA Today*. June 5, 2001. http://www.usatoday.com/news/ washington/june01/2001-06-06- daschle-linda.htm

A person who had aspirations of becoming a journalism school dean should know those passages needed attribution.

> *"I want to know why, under the Democratic leadership, some corporations are singled out for antitrust suits while other corporations – sometimes as large or larger – are totally ignored."*
> **The Savage Nation, page 204.**

Savage is talking about the antitrust suit brought by the government in the Clinton term against Microsoft, which it accused of trying to squelch competition by smaller companies. A federal judge eventually ruled in favor of the government.

But Savage rails on for a couple of pages about the "Liberal goons" that shook down Microsoft and chairman Bill Gates.

The point is, the feds started looking at Microsoft when George H.W. Bush – a Republican — was in office. It's silly to think that non-political government workers would drop an investigation just because the party holding the White House has changed.

> *"How many times did you hear the following:*
> *"Senator (Joseph) Lieberman is a very moral man. He's an orthodox (sic) Jew"? ... He is a hypocrite who uses his religious affiliation to push left-wing views, even though his political orientation conflicts with his religious orientation."* **The Savage Nation, page 207.**

This is from another screed Savage wrote in August 2000 to do his bit to derail the Gore-Lieberman ticket. Too bad he was so quick to judgment – he wrote this when Lieberman's selection by Gore was common knowledge, but not yet official – because not two weeks after Savage's column appeared on Newsmax, the *New York Times* ran an article with this quote: "Lieberman refers to himself as an 'observant Jew,' and not Orthodox. It is an intentional distinction that his staff laments has been overlooked in most of the coverage devoted to the first Jew to be nominated by one of the major two parties for vice president.

'He refers to himself as observant, as opposed to Orthodox, because he doesn't follow the strict Orthodox code and doesn't want to offend the Orthodox and his wife feels the same way,' said a Lieberman press officer who spoke on condition of ano-nymity."[30]

There was no correction submitted by Savage.

"Not long ago, a leader of the Democrat Party at-tended a seminar in Switzerland where Professor Peter Singer, distinguished scholar at "Youtha-nasia U." (Princeton), was among the honored speakers. Singer is distinguished not so much for his studies in euthanasia – the 'mercy' killing of

---

30 "Lieberman's specific form of Judaism is not easy to define, Candidate calls himself an 'Observant' Jew, rather than Orthodox," by Laurie Goodstein, *New York Times*, Aug. 25, 2000.

the elderly – but for his advocacy of 'youthana-sia,' the killing of handicapped youth, in former times known as infanticide." **The Savage Nation, page 208.**

This is a rewrite of a column Savage wrote in January, 2000, after the World Economic Forum in Davos, Switzerland. In the original column, Savage identified Clinton as that Democratic leader, and he also mentioned – grudgingly – that the "seminar" was about economics.

His omission of those two facts is not surprising, given Savage's penchant for ignoring that which does not further his point at the time. This time, rather than just indict Clinton for his presence at a seminar at which Singer was in attendance, Savage seeks to indict the entire Democratic Party.

What Savage neglects to mention, in both the column and the book, is that there were 1,500 delegates at this conference, comprised of politicians, academics and other world leaders. But Savage would have us believe that Clinton flew out to Switzerland, palled around with Peter Singer and talked about killing little babies over schnapps.

Are our country's leaders expected to bypass important world forums simply because their organizers did not vet their attendance lists with them?

Savage's attempt to stain all Democrats, by associating them with the questionable ideas of one person, falls flat once everything is out in the open.

*"Most of the red-state politicians fail to compre-
hend that the American people are behind them
and that the people want them to push through
Congress a real conservative agenda."*
Liberalism is a Mental Disorder, page XI

Typically, Savage gives no backup for this unproven assertion, which could be easily refuted. For example, a report written by Stan Greenberg and Bob Borosage of the Institute for America's Future about a week after the election, culled from the Joint National Post-Election Survey, showed just the opposite.

The two found that "… the public's priorities are wholly different than those the president put forth in the days after the election. That is particularly clear if one looks at fiscal and tax policies, health care, and Social Security privatization.

"The president has announced his intention to use his 'political capital' to forge ahead, perhaps boldly, in these areas, but he does so without a mandate from voters and without public support.

"The potential for a conservative overreach is considerable, as these issues are joined in the months ahead."[31]

Many Bush supporters, the two wrote, "disagree with the president's broader policy priorities and could easily pull back from the president during the policy debates ahead."

---

31 Stan Greenberg and Bob Borosage, "Re:What Mandate? A Report on the Joint National Post-Election Survey," Institute for America's Future, Nov. 11, 2004.

"In 2001-2002 (which are the latest available figures), the Association of Trial Lawyers of America was the Democrats' leading Political Action Committee donor, surpassing even the labor unions." **Liberalism is a Mental Disorder, page 104.**

I don't know where Savage got his figures for that claim because he did not footnote it. But, according to Open Secrets.org, in the 2002 election cycle (which I used because Savage's book was published in 2002), the Trial Lawyers Association gave the Democrats $3,941,088, making it the *10th* largest donor.

Among those donors higher on the list was the American Federation of Teachers, which donated slightly more than $5 million; the Laborers Union, which donated about $5.1 million; Communication Workers of America, which donated $5.5 million, the Carpenters and Joiners Union, which donated $6.1 million; Service Employees International Union, which donated $6.8 million, and the American Federation of State, County and Municipal Employees, which donated just more than $9 million.[32]

To buttress his argument against trial lawyers or, as he calls them, the briefcase mafia, Savage then goes on to quote a number of instances of ridiculous lawsuits which resulted in multi-million dollar settlements or jury judgments. Many of the argu-

---

32 Open Secrets.org:
    http://opensecrets.org/bigpicture/topcontribs.asp?cycle=2002

ments and examples come courtesy of Trial Lawyers Inc.com, a project of the Center for Legal Policy at the Manhattan Institute in New York. The Manhattan Institute is a conservative think tank that has advocated for such issues as deregulation of environmental and consumer issues and for school vouchers.

But Savage even botches it when he has the evidence right in front of him.

"Two short months after his call to solidarity, the most liberal member of the Senate was back on the road stirring up division." **Liberalism is a Mental Disorder, page 169.**

Savage cites as his source for his claim that U.S. Sen. John Kerry of Massachusetts is the "most liberal" Senator an article that appeared in the Feb. 28, 2004 issue of the National Journal, which purported to rank Senators in 2003, based on their votes.

The problem with that ranking, as FactCheck.org pointed out in October 2004, is that Kerry wasn't present for more than half of the 62 votes included in the rank because he was campaigning.

In addition, that ranking was based solely on economic issues, it did not rank him on social or foreign policy issues, therefore, it did not present a total picture.[33]

---

33 "How Liberal is John Kerry?" FactCheck.org:
    http://www.factcheck.org/article284.html

So while the Journal did rank Kerry as the "most liberal" Senator for 2003 – again, based only on economic issues – it also named him as the 11th most liberal Senator over his entire career.

FactCheck.org also notes that a vote analysis of 2003 Senate roll call votes by Prof. Keith T. Poole of the University of California at San Diego shows that Kerry is the 22nd most liberal US Senator.

Liberals and Education

"Today, of course, the teachers union has just about eliminated testing. They favor outcome-based 'learning,' which has more to do with the feelings of a student than with their grasp of knowledge." **The Savage Nation, page 2.**

I suppose Savage makes this statement to illustrate how the quality of education has eroded since the 1950s, and, of course, in Savage's nation, that is the fault of the teacher's union, the National Education Association. But his statement is just not true.

President George Bush signed his "No Child Left Behind" Act – one of the cornerstones of his first run for president — in January 2002. Savage's book was published about a year later, plenty of time for Savage to have researched that assertion.

If he had, he would have discovered that Bush's NCLB mandated new yearly testing for students in grades 3 to 8.[34] The

---

34 Fact Sheet: No Child Left Behind Act;
http://www.whitehouse.gov/news/releases/2002/01/20020108.html

program also mandates that schools meet yearly progress goals or risk a number of putative measures, including state takeover. Sounds pretty outcome-based to me.

Further, if Savage had bothered to read any of the NEA's stances on the issue, he would have discovered that the organization advocates not for less testing, as much as it does for smarter testing.

As the NEA's position paper on the issue states, "The issue is not to test or not to test. Students are subject to an array of standardized and teacher developed tests each year. The key question is, 'How do we help students achieve, rather than hurting them?' Instead of just applying more tests, NEA calls for smarter testing that also provides students and schools the tools they need to succeed."[35]

Among those tools: Improved tests and assessments. Nothing about "feelings" and everything about results.

> *During the Vietnam War, schools stopped teaching history in favor of lessons in white male crimes for ancient wrongdoings. Educators traded in their history books in favor of Tommy Has Two Mommies.* **The Savage Nation, page 28.**

Hmmm. The Vietnam War ended in 1973. The book "*Heath-*

---

35 NEA Issues in Education, "Testing Plus: Real Accountability with Real Results." http://www.nea.org/accountability/testplus.html

er Has Two Mommies" (emphasis mine) was published in 1990. So not only does Savage misstate the name of the book, he's wildly wrong about when it was published. All in the name of trying to prove his point.

> *"In California, teachers (starting with kindergar-ten) are being encouraged to teach that homosex-uality, bisexuality – and even transsexuality – is normal behavior."* **The Savage Nation, page 95.**

Savage references the California Student Safety and Violence Act of 2002, designed to protect students and staff from harassment due to their sexual orientation.

Contrary to Savage's inflammatory assertion, the bill does not "encourage" teachers to teach about homosexuality. Rather, it says that students and staff who happen to be gay or bi-sexual are protected.

As one California education official said, "The question is always, 'Where does that topic fit in with the curriculum of that particular course.' "[36]

> *"Just look at what the Novato, California, school board did in the fall of 2002. Literally in the*

---

36 "Policies for teachers differ; Local officials explain what can, can't be said about homosexuality in the classroom." *The Daily Review*, Aug. 19, 2002.

*middle of the night they approved the highly
controversial homosexual agenda video, 'That's
a Family!' for use with their fifth grade classes."*
The Enemy Within, pages 179-180.

Typical Savage misrepresentation of what really happened. The real facts didn't suit his purpose, so he twisted them to make them fit. Not surprisingly, the source Savage cites is Citizen Magazine, an imprint of Christian Nationalist James Dobson's "Focus on the Family" organization.

First of all, Savage clearly wants the implication to be that the Novato school board met in the middle of the night and passed this in secret. Of course, that's not what happened. The board voted only after a five-hour meeting, which had followed nearly a year of discussion and debate on the topic.

More than 300 people showed up at the meeting in August when the board decided to limit the film's use to fifth-grade health classes, which included sex education.[37]

And the one salient point Savage left out? According to a Dec. 18, 2002 article in the Marin Independent Journal, parents could opt out their children if they wanted to.

As far as Savage's claim that the movie is a "highly controversial homosexual agenda video," a discussion of gay couples comprises only a portion of its 35-minute running time. Also

---

37   http://www.fordfound.org/publications/ff_report/view_ff_report_
     detail.cfm?report_index=379

discussed are interracial parents, divorced parents, single parents and grandparents as guardians.

But all that doesn't make for good outrage.

> *"Liberal pressure groups are using strong-arm tactics on textbook manufacturers to remove language, ideas and traditions they find offensive."*
> **The Enemy Within, pages 182-183.**

Savage cites as his source a June 2, 2003 column from the *Contra Costa Times*, in which columnist Suzanne Pardington discusses a book called *The Language Police* by Diane Ravitch.

He omits the fact that Pardington notes that Ravitch blames the sanitizing of textbooks on "the politically correct left and the morally correct right."

Now, why wouldn't Savage want you to know that Right-wing groups are just as responsible for "textbook sanitizing" as groups on the left?

> *"While the throat-cutters in dirty nightshirts beheaded Americans, the clipped-hair czarinas of lower learning at a California middle school required students to pretend they were Muslims – including chanting and praying to Allah!*
> *"These clueless educators (who deny Jews and Christians the same right to pray in school) encouraged toleraaance (sic) for Muslims precisely*

at the same time many imams from the 'religion of peace' were assailing American infidels. Insanity!" **Liberalism is a Mental Disorder, page XXIII.**

Always the wannabe propagandist, Savage doesn't cite his source on this. However, in 2001, the Excelsior Middle School in Byron, Cal., had found itself embroiled in a controversy – shortly after the Sept. 11 attacks – over a lesson plan for the school's seventh graders.[38]

The plan encouraged kids to dress in Middle Eastern garb, recite Muslim prayers and basically immerse themselves in Muslim culture for three weeks. It was similar to a class on Christianity taught to the school's sixth graders, a part of the story which could have added some context and which Savage neglected to mention.

But, predictably, some parents overreacted, calling the lesson an "indoctrination" into Islam. Several filed suit against the district, but eventually lost. The case went all the way up to the 9th Circuit Court of Appeals in California, where an appeal filed by the plaintiffs was denied.

Now, Savage asserts that the children were learning about Islam in October 2001 when the "throat-cutters in dirty nightshirts" – one of his pet terms for Muslims – were beheading

---

38 Kelli A. Phillips, "Islam Lesson Lawsuit Disputed", *Contra Costa Times*, Jan. 10, 2003, Page C1.

Americans. But according to a Sept. 22, 2004 article in *USA Today* (Beheadings 'Theater of Terror' Amplifes Insurgents' Message), the beheadings didn't begin until May, 2004.

As he does in so many other instances, Savage goes over the top to drive home his point -- creating a fabrication along the way, when he didn't have to if he'd had confidence in the strength of his argument.

Sex

"Look at the epidemic of sexually transmitted diseases and the costs to society. Americans must fork over nearly twenty billion dollars annually in taxes at the federal, state and local levels just to pay for the consequences of sex outside marriage. That, my friend, no longer makes sex a 'private' matter. Not when you reach into my pocket to pick up the prices of teen pregnancy, STDs, and government-subsidized day care."

The Savage Nation, page 96.

It's hard to even know where to begin with this one. Savage, as usual, doesn't cite his sources for the $20 billion figure. And where's the evidence that all STDs are caused by sex outside marriage? Or that "government-subsidized day care" is used only by people who had children "outside" marriage? It's not there because it's not there.

Savage focuses on teenagers in this section, so one can safely assume that the numbers he gives relate to teenage sex. On that basis, he's wrong.

According to a study published in the journal *Perspectives on Sexual and Reproductive Health*, the total estimated cost for the 9 million new cases of STDs among people aged 15 to 24 years, reported in 2000, was $6.5 million.[39]

That same study estimated the total cost of STDs among all age groups in the 1990s to be between $9.3 billion and $15.5 billion.

So, even giving Savage the benefit of the doubt and stretching the point that $15.5 million is "nearly" $20 billion, Savage's claim still falls apart because there's no breakdown provided as to how much of that cost is due to STDs incurred "outside" marriage.

> *"San Francisco is one of the porno capitals of the world. There are a lot of little sex shops around, and I've poked my head into a few of them from time to time. Remember, I'm a social commentator. I'm an observer of what goes on in my country. That means I look at a lot of things, from high to low.*

---

39 "The Estimated Direct Medical Cost of Sexually Transmitted Diseases Among American Youth, 2000," *Perspectives on Sexual and Reproductive Health*, Vol. 36, No. 1, Jan./Feb. 2004: http://www.guttmacher.org/pubs/journals/3601104.html

I usually walk out of the lobby nauseated. I tell you, over the fifteen years that I've been looking into these places, I've seen American porn approach a level that is lower than pre-Hitler Germany." **The Savage Nation, page 103.**

It's hard to determine here whether Savage is arguing that pornography is getting more degrading, or if he's complaining that modern pornography isn't as good as it was in the 1930s.

Ok, I admit it. I included this purely for my own amusement. But check this out: *The Savage Nation* was published in 2002, and Savage began his radio career in 1994, when he served as a fill-in host. By his own admission, then, Savage has been "researching" San Francisco porn shops since 1987, seven years before going into radio. And, as he reveals in the paragraphs which follow the excerpt above, he also closely studied Japanese pornography and porn in Germany leading up to Hitler's rise to power. Isn't it interesting that he keeps getting nauseated, yet he still goes back? I tell you, this man is downright *devoted* to his research. Yeah, that's it. Research.

"Now, you should know that I'm a man who loves to study the genesis of words. This will astonish you. Take the origin of the word 'testimony.' If you break it down, 'testimony' goes back to the word 'testify' which, in turn, has as its Latin root the word 'testis. 'What other English word de-

*rives its meaning from testis? Testicle. The repro-
ductive gland of a male."* **The Enemy Within,
page 138.**

Savage follows that quote with a story he was told during the time he was traipsing through the tropics looking for herbs. He was told that males in a primitive tribe in New Guinea would greet each other by cupping their testicles in each other's hands. They did this, he said, to see if the other person was lying when he was talking.

Uh huh.

Anyway, Savage may be a botanist, but he's no etymologist. Looks like there's more than one "root" for testimony: According to Oxford, the root of testimony is the Latin *testimonium*.

And Savage says Liberals are obsessed with sex.

Islam and Muslims (and why they hate us)

"You see, it's not our foreign policy the Arabic world hates. It's our social pollution Muslim terrorists are rebelling against ... Hear me. It is the filth and pollution of our entertainment industry wafting across the world they despise." **The Enemy Within, page 88.**

"If you want to understand the war between Islam and Western civilization and why we are so hated, I believe it almost boils down to one word: sex. You see, for a traditional Arab like Osama bin Laden, this jihad is as much a battle about sexual license as it is anything else." **The Enemy Within, page 89.**

The ignorance displayed in those statements is absolutely stunning. So Osama bin Laden ordered the destruction of the World Trade Center, the Pentagon and who knows what else because of "Sex and the City"?

For a reality check, let's see what Bin Laden has to say.

In a March 1997 interview with CNN, Bin Laden said the following:

> *"We declared jihad against the US government, because the US government is unjust, criminal and tyrannical. It has committed acts that are extremely unjust, hideous and criminal whether directly or through its support of the Israeli occupation."*

> *"For this and other acts of aggression and in-justice, we have declared jihad against the US, because in our religion it is our duty to make jihad so that God's word is the one exalted to the heights and so that we drive the Americans away from all Muslim countries. As for what you asked whether jihad is directed against US soldiers, the civilians in the land of the Two Holy Places (Saudi Arabia, Mecca and Medina) or against the civilians in America, we have focused our declaration on striking at the soldiers in the country of The Two Holy Places."[40]*

Nothing in there about Hollywood or the entertainment

---

40 http://www.pbs.org/wgbh/pages/frontline/shows/binladen/

industry or sex. Where Savage gets this stuff is beyond me, because there's no citation to back up his argument. He seems to have an obsessive hatred for celebrities and some real issues with sex.

> *"Like Christianity, Islam spread quickly. But unlike Christianity, Islam spread through violent conquest. With swords, not sacraments."*
> **Liberalism is a Mental Disorder, page 35.**

This merits only a quickie. Ever hear of the Crusades? How about the Spanish Inquisition? Oh, but wait. Savage does mention – however obliquely, the Spanish Inquisition a page later:

> *"While the Spanish knights during the glory days of Spain drove the Islamofascists out, today's inherited class of weaklings are too busy in the discotheques at night to stand up and fight for their homeland."* **Liberalism is a Mental Disorder, page 36.**

See, when the "good guys" do it, they're driving out the Islamofascists.

When the Muslims do it, they're conquering and pillaging. Excellent propagandizing. Although, it probably would have stood up a little better if he hadn't put the two sections so close together.

"Listen to Winston Churchill, that political states-man who exposed communism's threat to the West. In his analysis, Islam, 'which above all other was founded and propagated by the sword – the tenets and principles of which are ... incentives to slaughter and which in three continents had produced fighting breeds of men – simulates a wild and merciless fanaticism.' "**Liberalism is a Mental Disorder, page 37.**

The endnote identifies this quote as having come from Churchill's famous "Sinews of Peace" speech given March 5, 1946 at Westminster College in Fulton, Mo. This is the speech in which Churchill coined the phrase "Iron Curtain," and which is noted by Churchill historians as the start of the Cold War.

The problem is, Churchill never uttered those words that fine day in Missouri.

Savage lifted that quote from an article written by Dr. John Hagee – pastor of Cornerstone Church in San Antonio, Texas – in WorldNetDaily.com (one of Savage's favorite news sources) on Aug. 30, 2002[41] and attributed it to Churchill's famous Westminster speech.

Hagee mentions the Westminster speech in the next paragraph, so there is the potential that someone could have read that passage quickly and misunderstood the attribution.

---

41 "ACLU assaults constitution,"WorldNetDaily, Aug. 30, 2002. http://worldnetdaily.com/news/article.asp?ARTICLE_ID=28781

The quote actually came from Churchill's first book, *The Story of the Malakand Field Force*, first published in 1898.

And, he got it wrong. The last line really reads "*stimulates* (emphasis mine. Savage wrote "simulates") a wild and merciless fanatacism."

Which means, of course, that Savage didn't bother to check the source.

> *"Every single major terrorist attack against the United States has been committed by radical Muslims."* **Liberalism is a Mental Disorder, page 37.**

Savage writes that in the same paragraph as his assurance that his book "is not a blanket condemnation of Islam or all Muslims."

He then attempts to refute anticipated arguments that Timothy McVeigh, the upstate New York man who blew up the Murrah federal office building in Oklahoma City in 1995, was a "Christian" terrorist. Savage argues that McVeigh was an "avowed agnostic."

In what's become typical Savage fashion, he sets up a false choice. In trying to divert the refutation of a point he made by inventing a specious argument that could be used against it, he shows why that argument is flawed (which he of course knew from the get-go), and then moves on to another point. As if by proving that McVeigh was not a "Christian" terrorist, his blow-ing up the Murrah building is therefore not considered a terrorist act.

Not so fast. The Oxford American Dictionary defines terrorist as "a person who uses terrorism in the pursuit of political gains." No mention of any religion there.

Here's some history: According to Oxford, "terrorist" was first applied to the Jacobins in the French Revolution, who advocated repression and violence in the pursuit of equality and democracy. Hmmmm. Anyway, the point is, McVeigh may not have been a Christian, but he wasn't a Muslim, either, so Savage lied yet again, when he wrote that Muslims committed all major terrorist attacks against the U.S.

Who would argue that the Murrah bombing, in which 168 men, women and children were killed, was not a major homeland terrorist attack? Until September 11th, the Murrah bombing was singularly considered to be the worst terrorist attack on U.S. soil.

And what about Eric Rudolph, the anti-abortion bomber who killed two people and wounded about 120 others in a three-state rampage? He would certainly be qualified as a terrorist ...

> *"Where's the outcry from the peace-loving, moderate mullahs when fellow Muslims murder children in cold blood? Why the silence? Why no outcry? There was hardly a peep of protest coming*

*from the mosques around the world. Have these
'moderate' Muslims become at least an accessory
to the crime because of their silence?"*
Liberalism is a Mental Disorder, page 43.

What could be more heart-wrenching and enraging than ignoring such inhumane acts of murdering innocent children?

Trouble is for Savage, Muslims around the word didn't ignore the massacre by Chechen separatists of hundreds of school children in 2004 in Beslan, Russia, which is to what he is referring.

Imams from around the world condemned the attack in no uncertain terms. Even Mohammed Mahdi Akef, the leader of the Muslim Brotherhood, the largest Islamic group in Egypt, called the killing of the children unjustified.

"What happened is not jihad [holy war] because Islam obligates us to respect the souls of human beings; it is not about taking them away," Akef said.[42]

Grand Sheik Mohammed Sayed Tantawi, Egypt's leading Muslim cleric, said, "What is the guilt of those children? Why should they be responsible for your conflict with the government? You are taking Islam as a cover and it is a deceptive cover; those who carry out the kidnappings are criminals, not Muslims."[43]

---

42 "Muslim leaders condemn killings," *Guardian Unlimited*, Sept. 5, 2004.
    http://www.guardian.co.uk/chechnya/Story/0,2763,1297682,00.html
43 Ibid

And then there's this, as reported in the Sydney Morning Herald: "Virtually all Arab governments and Iran put aside any Chechen sympathies and condemned the hostage-taking and later carnage in Beslan. King Abdullah II of Jordan, who was visiting President Vladimir Putin in Russia last week, called the siege 'criminal and cowardly'.

"The Saudi daily Arab News blasted Mr. Putin but saved its harshest condemnation for the guerrillas, 'who had put themselves in a position where no one would shed tears when the punishment came. They reached a new low when they chose toddlers as bargaining chips.' "[44]

Sounds like outrage to me, and typical Savage ignorance of the facts.

Savage follows that with another ... curious ... argument.
"Remember when the Catholic Church was confronted with 'a handful' of cases of sexual abuse by pedophiliac priests in Boston? The Righteous Ones in the media were quick to demand the head of Cardinal Bernard Law served on a platter. His crime? Neglect. ... The guy did the right thing and stepped down to make things right. Fine.

---

44 "Terrorists incite rising disgust in Arab states," *The Sydney Morning Herald*, Sept. 6, 2004. http://www.smh.com.au/articles/2004/09/05/1094322644860.html

"But, there's a huge difference between neglecting to do your job and slicing the throats of fellow humans. So, let's connect the dots. When Muslim terrorists slashed and then paraded around with the heads of innocent victims, literally, the media's Righteous Ones were AWOL. ... Do you see what's going on here? All Christians bad, but only Muslim terrorists bad." **Liberalism is a Mental Disorder, pages 43-44.**

First thing's first: Not six pages earlier, Savage wrote that his book was "not a blanket condemnation of Islam or all Muslims ... I'll be the first to say that Islam doesn't kill people, — Islamists do." He completely contradicts that statement in the paragraph above. Which is it, sloppy thought patterns or just sloppy proofreading? Or is he just a liar?

As for the argument that he tries to make ... well, I'm not even sure what his point is. That reporting about one of the biggest scandals in modern Catholic history automatically equals condemning all Christians just stretches all credulity. This is a prime example of the propagandist technique known as sweeping generalizations. The task of the propagandist is to present arguments that win over readers, not make wild assertions that your critics can pick apart with ease.

"Depending on who's counting, Muhammad (sic) had between sixteen and twenty-two wives ... not

including concubines. His youngest wife, Aisha 1, was six years old, which in every state, with the possible exception of Massachusetts, would make him a pedophile." **Liberalism is a Mental Disorder, page 45.**

The age of Aisha at the time of her marriage, and at the time of the marriage's consummation, is apparently not as cut-and-dried as Savage would have us believe. Depending on who does the research (which, by the way, dates back to at least the 1920s), she was anywhere from 10 or 12 to 19, a dispute Savage fails to mention.[45]

"Another fact concealed by the followers of Islam is that there are actually two versions of the Ko-ran: the fundamentalist, hard-core Arabic edi-tion and the watered-down, coffeehouse-blended English tea translation." **Liberalism is a Mental Disorder, page 45.**

In this passage, Savage references the same Hagee column in World Net Daily from which he lifted the misattributed Churchill quote discussed earlier. Hagee was writing about how the University of North Carolina in 2002 required its first-year students to read a book by Prof. Michael Sells called *Approach-ing the Qur'an.* Some people objected and took the university to

---

45 "Age of Aisha at Time of Marriage,": http://www.muslim.org/islam/aishe-age.htm

court. The American Civil Liberties Union defended the university, which drew Hagee's ire.

Had Savage bothered to look into the issue, he would have discovered that Sells' book is not a "watered-down" version of the Quran. Instead, it simply presents about 35 "suras," or chapters, found at the end of the Quran, meant to give people a general idea of what Islam is about.[46]

Savage's argument is therefore weakened because he chooses to ignore details like these.

> *"What amazes me is the screaming silence coming from the women's movement, especially in light of how these Islamofascists treat their females."* **Liberalism is a Mental Disorder, page 45.**

Apparently, Savage doesn't get out much. A number of feminist groups routinely speak out about the rights of Muslim women, not the least of which are the Feminist majority Foundation (www.feminist.org), and the National Organization for Women (www.now.org).

> *"According to published reports, Abu Hamza al-Masri, a radical Islamic clerk, urges Muslim women to 'breed children for the purpose of cre-*

---

46 White Cloud Press.
    http://www.caveatpress.com/product.asp?specific=jnpqhsfo

ating suicide bombers." **Liberalism is a Mental Disorder, page 46.**

There's enough written about al Masri, called Britain's most radical Muslim cleric, without having to repeat things that are baseless. Savage's footnote references a WorldNetDaily.com article from October, 2004[47], that talks about the secretly recorded tapes made by Abu Hamza al Masri for devoted followers. But in the tape quoted, al Masri talks about a mother who encouraged her son to be a suicide bomber. There's nothing in the article, aside from the first paragraph – which offers no backup – that quotes al Masri telling women to breed children to become bombers.

Predictably, this story was picked up and run as gospel by a number of Right-wing blogs. But even the mainstream British press writing about the tapes do not mention the odd claim. Most, such as the *Times of London*, talk about al Masri's call for bombers to work locally.[48]

A quick final note on page 46: Savage condemns "Muhammad's" followers for being "some of the worst homophobes on the planet." He cites a "Hadith" – quotes that some followers attribute to Muhammad – where Muhammad purportedly said that homosexuals should be stoned.

---

47 "Muslim cleric urges 'women of mass destruction' ", WorldNetDaily.com, Oct. 9, 2004.
    http://www.wnd.com/news/article.asp?ARTICLEID=40832
48 "Detectives study audio tapes that urge attacks," *Times of London*, April 27, 2004.

Granted, there are Islamic countries, such as Iran, where gays are executed. But the very footnote cited by Savage could refute his argument, had he printed the entire passage.

Savage cites some text from a Web site called Religious Tolerance (www.religioustolerance.org), which quotes the Hadith.

However, the passage goes on to say, "Traditionalist orthodox Muslims generally claim that the Hadith literature contains the authentic sayings of Muhammad. Many liberal Muslims doubt the authenticity of at least some of them. The latter might point out that during the times of the first Caliphs, Muslims did not know what to do with individuals guilty of "liwat/lutiyya." No sahabi (companion) of Muhammad could quote a saying or decision of Muhammad relating to this question.[49]

At any rate, isn't it somewhat ironic that Savage – one of whose most infamous quotes came when he told a purportedly gay viewer of his short-lived television show on MSNBC to "get AIDS and die, you pig," and to choke on a sausage – should denounce homophobes?

> *"The Islamic penetration marches on, this time*
> *dividing the close-knit, Polish-Catholic town of*
> *Hamtramck, Michigan. There, residents were*
> *forced by the Islam-influenced town council to*
> *'endure Muslim calls to prayer in Arabic broad-*

---

49 "Islam and Sexuality," ReligiousTolerance.org.
    http://www.religioustolerance.org/hom_isla.htm

*cast over loudspeaker six times a day.' The
Muslims claim their decree is no different from
a Christian church signaling parishioners with
church bells.
"They're wrong. Church bells are a voluntary
call to worship which takes place behind closed
doors. Imagine the uproar by the keepers of the
media if Father Fred conducted mass over the
loudspeakers six times a day."* **Liberalism is a
Mental Disorder, page 48.**

Savage gets it wrong again. Had he bothered to read any of
the articles written about the controversy, rather than rely on
the third-hand reporting published in the Right-wing Front-
PageMagazine.com, he would have found that even those opposed to allowing the calls to prayer recognized they couldn't
stop it.[50] The controversy was over making the calls a part of the
town's noise ordinance.

Even his argument is flawed. The ordinance was simply to
allow the two-minute calls to prayer over loudspeakers, not the
actual prayers, as Savage implies.

*"The Islamofascists are today, right now, plot-
ting a nuclear attack on our country. According*

---

[50] "Islamic call to prayer stirs tension; immigrant Muslims in a
traditionally Polish town in Michigan run into opposition from their
Christian neighbors," *Chicago Tribune*, April 21, 2004.

*to one of the world's foremost terrorism experts,
our Islamofascist enemies have the capability to
do so: Yossef Bodansky is on record saying that
Islamic terrorists have a suitcase nuke."*
Liberalism is a Mental Disorder, page 49.

Savage cites an article from the Oct. 5, 2004 issue of News-max.com, in which Bodansky is interviewed. In it, he says, "There is ample evidence from impeccable sources that the Islamist-Jihadist forces are adamant on striking out before the U.S. elections. Some of the warnings specify a commitment to inflicting mass casualties on an unprecedented scale, perhaps through the use of a nuclear suitcase-bomb (which they definitely have)."

Notice he said "perhaps." Savage is incapable of subtlety.

He also didn't bother to provide the rest of the quote: "At the same time, however, the key terrorism sponsoring states urge prudence, fearing U.S. retribution. Right now, there are intense theological deliberations within the Islamist movement about what to do next. We will surely see the outcome of these deliberations."

So Bodansky seems to equivocate. But Savage does not include Bodansky's equivocation. What a shock.

Once again calling for "moderate" Muslim leaders to condemn acts of terrorism -- specifically the Beslan, Russia, school massacre -- and deriding those who he feels have not gone far enough, Savage writes:

"Or the bogus words of 'grief' offered by the public relations arm of God knows who, the Council on American-Islamic Relations (CAIR): 'No words can describe the horror and grief generated by the deaths of so many innocent people at the hands of those who dishonor the cause they espouse. We offer sincere condolences to the families of the victims and call for a swift resolution to the conflict in the troubled region.' "These pronouncements are nothing more than 'donor preservation' tactics … notice CAIR didn't even have the courage to call the kidnappers Muslims." **Liberalism is a Mental Disorder, page 53.**

Savage doesn't cite his source for that quote, but it's a fair bet that he didn't get it from CAIR's Web site. Because if he did, he would have seen the very next *paragraph*, (but there's always the possibility he ignored it):

"CAIR recently launched an online petition drive, called 'Not in the Name of Islam,' designed to disassociate Islam from the violent acts of a few Muslims. The 'Not in the Name of Islam' petition states: 'We, the undersigned Muslims, wish to state clearly that those who commit acts of terror, murder and cruelty in the name of Islam are not only destroying innocent lives, but are also betraying the values of the faith they claim to represent.

'No injustice done to Muslims can ever justify the massacre of innocent people, and no act of terror will ever serve the cause of Islam. We repudiate and dissociate ourselves from any Muslim group or individual who commits such brutal and un-Islamic acts. We refuse to allow our faith to be held hostage by the criminal actions of a tiny minority acting outside the teachings of both the Quran and the Prophet Muhammad, peace be upon him.' "[51]

---

51 "CAIR condemns school killings in Russia," Sept. 7, 2004.
http://www.cairnet.org/default.asp?Page=articleView&id=
1200&theType=NR

Anti-War Liberals and the War on Terror

"Well, the peaceniks might as well get in the boxcars now. The fact of the matter is, war does bring peace. Look at World War II. The idiots don't even know their own history. Hitler was killed. That was the end of the war. And the war brought fifty years of peace, more or less."
The Savage Nation, page 54.

War brings peace? Savage obviously doesn't subscribe to the theory that World War I begat World War II.

And 50 years of peace? I guess the Korean War, the Vietnam War and the Gulf War don't count.

Savage really hates antiwar activists. He has called them un-American. In *The Savage Nation*, for example, he unequivocally states that antiwar protesters can "be detained for aiding and abetting the enemy under the laws governing sedition." (Page 55).

That's up for interpretation. First of all, there is no law against sedition, per se. According to the Columbia Encyclopedia, Sixth Edition, "The libel decision of Sullivan v. New York Times (1964), by granting special protection to criticism of public officials, largely eliminated what remained of the crime of sedition in the United States." (Find it at http://www.bartleby.com/65/se/sedition.html).

It's now called seditious conspiracy. Under Sect. 2384 of USC 18, Part 1, Chapter 115[52], "Seditious Conspiracy" is defined as:

"If two or more persons in any State or Territory, or in any place subject to the jurisdiction of the United States, conspire to overthrow, put down, or to destroy by force the Government of the United States, or to levy war against them, or to oppose by force the authority thereof, or by force to prevent, hinder, or delay the execution of any law of the United States, or by force to seize, take, or possess any property of the United States contrary to the authority thereof, they shall each be fined under this title or imprisoned not more than twenty years, or both."

Section 2388 deals with activities against the military in a time of war. They are defined as:

"(a) Whoever, when the United States is at war, willfully makes or conveys false reports or false statements with intent to interfere with the operation or success of the military or

---

52 US Code, Title 18: caselaw.lp.findlaw.com/casecode/uscodes/18/parts/
    i/chapters/115/toc.html

naval forces of the United States or to promote the success of its enemies; or Whoever, when the United States is at war, willfully causes or attempts to cause insubordination, disloyalty, mutiny, or refusal of duty, in the military or naval forces of the United States, or willfully obstructs the recruiting or enlistment service of the United States, to the injury of the service or the United States, or attempts to do so Shall be fined under this title or imprisoned not more than twenty years, or both.

"(b) If two or more persons conspire to violate subsection (a) of this section and one or more such persons do any act to effect the object of the conspiracy, each of the parties to such conspiracy shall be punished as provided in said subsection (a).

"(c) Whoever harbors or conceals any person who he knows, or has reasonable grounds to believe or suspect, has committed, or is about to commit, an offense under this section, shall be fined under this title or imprisoned not more than ten years, or both.

"(d) This section shall apply within the admiralty and maritime jurisdiction of the United States, and on the high seas, as well as within the United States."

Neither of these sections are so cut-and-dried as to support Savage's blanket statement.

Apparently, Savage would run the country the same way he runs his radio program. Agree with what he says and he'll keep you on all night. Disagree with him, or tell him he's wrong, and he'll cut you off, insult you and then hang up on you.

"Here's another word game coming from the left wing. They assert the only way to deal with terrorism is to address the root causes. Let me decode what they're really saying. You are the root cause ... For this reason, the Red Diaper Doper Babies reason you shouldn't have a civilization." **The Savage Nation, page 66.**

Savage simply substitutes his own "word game" in this passage.

What those on the left actually have said, in terms of getting to the "root" of the problem, is that continued American military presence in Arabic holy lands has inflamed Muslim passions against us. Bin Laden is on record as saying as much. It's as simple as that. I have never heard anyone on the left advocate abandoning our "civilization" as a way to stop Islamic terrorism.

"I spoke with former Israeli Prime Minister Benjamin Netanyahu about terrorism. He artfully traced modern terrorism from the 'hateful ideology' of Nazism to what we're seeing today on the world scene, with its implications for America. One clear difference surfaced. The Germans under Hitler were not willing to blow themselves up with munitions." **The Savage Nation, page 66.**

Well, not exactly. According to a report in the *Intelligence*

Bulletin of June 1946,[53] there was a movement in the German ranks to create a Japanese-like Kamikaze unit in the Luftwaffe.

The Intelligence Bulletin was published regularly throughout World War II by the Military Intelligence Service. Its purpose was to give enlisted men and officers the latest information on the enemy's tactics and equipment.

According to the report:

"In fact, there is much evidence to indicate that the Nazi suicidists were laying their plans long before their Japanese allies conceived the idea for this unconventional tactic. Only bureaucratic inefficiency, and disinterest in official circles as high as Hitler himself, forestalled the appearance of Nazi Kamikazes in the air over Normandy on D-day."

So much for that theory.

"Richard Beske, William Christison, Kathleen McGrath Christison, Ray Close, Patrick Eddington, David MacMichael, and Raymond McGovern make up their (Veteran Intelligence Professionals for Sanity) steering committee. I didn't know we had so many anti-war generals and intelligence personnel. No wonder our military stank under Clinton." **The Enemy Within, page 85.**

---

53 "The German Kamikazes," *The Intelligence Bulletin*, June, 1946: http://www.lonesentry.com/articles/kamikaze/index.html

Savage is in prime form over the next 15 or so paragraphs, ridiculing "retired General So-and-So" who, in Savage's scenario, is knocking around in his garage, waiting for a major news outlet to call for their take on terrorists. He's referring to the people he names, but the thing is, none of them were military generals. They were all ex-CIA people.

> *"As if these out-to-pasture infidels would know more about the Afghanistan or Iraqi conflict than, say, Secretary of Defense Rumsfeld."* **The Enemy Within, page 85.**

Now, had Savage done even a minimal amount of checking into his targets, he would have known that some of them *would* know more about Middle Eastern conflicts than Rumsfeld.

Take Raymond Close, for example. A former CIA analyst, Close started his career in the Middle East in the late 1930s, including living in Arab and Muslim countries for 37 years.[54] *Slightly* more experience on the subject than Rumsfeld, I'd say.

> *"On January 30, 2005, Iraq held their first free election in fifty years. Without question this is a great victory for democracy. More than 70 percent of eligible Iraqi voters – 95 percent in several Baghdad neighborhoods – yes, Iraqis by the*

---

54 http://www.pbs.org/wgbh/pages/frontline/shows/binladen/bombings/close.html

millions, braved suicide bombings and threats of mayhem to register their vote for freedom." **Liberalism is a Mental Disorder, page 1.**

Actually, according to final results released by the Iraqi election committee, the turnout was 58 percent.[55] The higher numbers were released early in the process, before actual counts were made and the results were certified. But the earlier, higher numbers made for a better success story from the Right wing's point of view.

> *"... Bush got trapped trying to fight a politically correct war while America's Marxist media militia, armed with zoom lenses, waited to pounce on any PC violation. ...*
> *"That said, here's a prime example of their trick-ledown PC stupidity. As the coalition troops were preparing for battle, one lieutenant colonel who shall remain nameless advised those under his command: 'Iraq is steeped in history. It is the site of the Garden of Eden, of the Great Flood and the birthplace of Abraham. Tread lightly there.'*
> *"How exactly does an Abrams tank tread light-ly?"* **Liberalism is a Mental Disorder, page 3.**

Well, even though Savage says the speaker will remain

---

55   "Shiite alliance wins plurality in Iraq," CNN.com. Feb. 14, 2005

anonymous, he identifies him in the chapter's endnotes as Lt. Col. Tim Collins. Collins was in charge of the 1st Battalion, Royal Irish Guards. Irish. As in United Kingdom. The propagandist ignores context if a good quote will help him prove his point. Savage is trying to make the point that "America's Marxist media militia" compromised the *American* military; he would not have been able to use that quote and make his snarky comment if he had identified the speaker as a British officer.

By the way, isn't it interesting that Savage would have such strong opinions on the military, having himself spent the Vietnam era picking berries and herbs in the South Pacific?

Colleges and Universities

"A report conducted by the American Council of Trustees and Alumni in February of 2002 found that anti-war rallies protesting our involvement in Afghanistan were hosted on more than 140 college campuses in some thirty-six states. The report concluded 'many professors and administrators are quick to clamp down on acts of patriotism, such as flying the American flag, and look down on students who question the professors' 'politically correct' ideas in class.'" **The Enemy Within, page 82.**

As if the reader couldn't tell the bias in the referenced study, Savage neglects to mention that Lynn Cheney, wife of the Vice President, is among the organization's founders. Check it out for yourself at www.goacta.org. Click on the "mission" link. Savage often cites studies done by groups with vested interests in the topics without divulging those inherent conflicts of interest.

In writing about University of Colorado Professor Ward Churchill, who gained notoriety for his outspokenness against the US and his seeming support of the 9/11 attackers:

> *"In case there was any dispute over his ant-American position, he told Satya magazine in April 2004: 'I want the ... U.S. off the planet. Out of existence altogether.' Clearly, such a maniacal ranting can only be explained as a byproduct of the mental disorder of liberalism."* **Liberalism is a Mental Disorder, page XXIV.**

That ellipsis is important. The full quote, in proper context, is:

"If I defined the state as being the problem, just what happens to the state? I've never fashioned myself to be a revolutionary, but it's part and parcel of what I'm talking about. You can create through consciousness a situation of flux, perhaps, which something better can replace it. In instability there's potential.

"That's about as far as I go with revolutionary consciousness I'm actually a de-evolutionary. I don't want other people in charge of the apparatus of the state as the outcome of a socially transformative process that replicates oppression. I want the state gone: transform the situation to U.S. out of North America. U.S. off the planet. Out of existence altogether."[56]

Like most of the quotes Savage uses to buttress his argu-

---

56 *Satya Magazine*, http://www.satyamag.com/apr04/churchill.html

ments, this one is ripe for interpretation and not black-and-white, as Savage would have his readers believe. Here's mine: Churchill is advocating for the abolition of "the state" as a general term; he uses the term "U.S." to describe the apparatus, not the people. He wants a society in which there is no overriding central authority, but, rather, one in which many sub-societies exist along with one another, somewhat similar to Native American society before the settlement of Indian lands.

A popular point of view? Probably not, but it's certainly not "maniacal ranting." But Savage often attempts to distort the meaning of a quote by leaving out its key parts, then expounding on the sliver of information he deigns to give his reader.

Prisoners
and Prisons

"As of this writing, Horacio's chances are excellent he'll be placed ahead of the 57,000 law-abiding citizens in the country who are praying for a desperately needed kidney transplant." **The Enemy Within, page 66.**

Savage is referring to Horacio Reyes-Camarena, an Oregon death row inmate who was receiving dialysis treatments while his lawyers pursued his appeals. Doctors at the prison hospital convinced him that he would be better served with a kidney transplant. The procedure would also cost Oregon taxpayers less, they reasoned.

Savage gets the facts right until he makes the statement I quoted. Nowhere in the article Savage cites is there any indication of Reyes-Camarena's chances of getting a transplant ahead of those already on the transplant list.

And frankly, Savage's use of the 57,000 people waiting for kidney transplants is a little misleading in that not everybody gets an organ based on where they fall on the list. Geography, age and whether the patient would be a match for the donor also play into the decision of who gets which organ.

As it turned out, Reyes-Camarena's bid for a transplant was turned down in June, 2003.[57]

---

57 "State rejects Transplant for Death Row Inmate," *The Los Angeles Times,* June 17, 2003

HIV
and AIDS

"In fact, more American adults, ages 25-44, die from heart disease, cancer and suicide than from AIDS." **The Enemy Within, page 60.**

Savage cites 1998 data presented in the 2000-2001 CDC Fact Book (a copy of which can be viewed at http:// usa.usembassy.de/etexts/tech/cdc.pdf), which was released in September 2000. On the surface, the statistics Savage cites are true, but they don't completely support his contention. For example, the report notes that while 43.5 percent of non-Hispanic blacks who die between the ages of 25 and 44 die from heart disease, 43.3 percent die from HIV/AIDS. So while Savage is technically correct, the distinction he fails to note significantly weakens his argument.

Statistics among Hispanics in that age group somewhat turn Savage's assertion on its ear: 16.8 percent die from cancer, 10.3 percent die from heart disease and 21.1 percent die from HIV.

"According to the Centers for Disease Control, this 'private activity' has created a 17.7 percent jump in new HIV cases since 1999 among gay/ bi/tri men." **The Enemy Within, page 128.**

Savage is quoting here from a July 28, 2003 article posted by the Reuters news service about a three-year increase in the number of men diagnosed with HIV. By "private activity," he means gay sex.

Apparently he stopped reading after the quote, because if he continued into the article, he would have read this:

"But CDC officials cautioned that the increase could have been caused by more men being tested for the virus and was not proof that gays and bisexuals were being infected more quickly.

"They also noted that the data could be skewed because it did not include New York, California and other states with large HIV-infected populations, but said it does have value because it reflects what is happening in 25 states."[58]

---

58 http://www.aegis.org/news/re/2003/RE030745.html

The Liberal Supreme Court, and Other 'Liberal Activist' Judges

"If Osama was one day delivered to us alive, and if the radical leftist Rats who hate America have their way, OBL will not stand trial before a military tribunal. Instead, his 'case' would probably be presented to Judge Ginsberg, formerly of the ACLU."

"... And, of course, Osama would skirt the death penalty. He'd probably be released for good behavior, sentenced to do one hundred hours of community service lecturing Americans on the wonders of Islam at Harvard's Kennedy School of Government (that ghetto of radicalism where Hollywood Idiots are often guest lecturers)."

The Savage Nation, page 61.

Throughout his trilogy, Savage regularly indulges himself in flights of fancy such as the preceding two paragraphs. We'll never know if he actually believes what he writes, but it certainly is an effective way to agitate the masses.

First of all, how absurd a notion to think that a sitting Supreme Court Justice would be directly involved in the criminal trial of Osama bin Laden, no matter how Savage meant "presented." Does Savage truly believe the Constitution would be bent for some "Liberal agenda?"

And concerning the second paragraph, does any reasonable person really believe that bin Laden would not be convicted of whatever crime with which he was charged? Savage is simply trotting out the old canard that Liberals are "soft on crime." But it's quite the hot-button to push, especially in these days of the "Global War on Terror."

> *"In fact, in her capacity as the ACLU's top legal dog for the better part of a decade, Ruthie co-authored a misguided and dangerous report ("Sex Bias in the U.S. Code") which actually recommended the age of consent for sexual activity be lowered to just 12 years of age."* **The Enemy Within, page 28.**

Savage uses that passage as his introduction to a several-paragraphs-long denunciation of Supreme Court Justice Ruth Bader Ginsberg and the American Civil Liberties Union. He goes on to say that Ginsberg, in the aforementioned report, "believes prostitution should be legalized," that "all-boy and all-girl groups should be sexually integrated, and women should be part of the military draft and assigned to combat duty." And as his source, does he cite the report? Of course not! Instead, he cites a third-hand review of the report written by Phyllis Schlafly, the Grande Dame of the Right-wing. Schlafly wrote about the report in an early 1990s edition of her "Phyllis Schlafly Report" that, as of March 2006, was not available in her online archives.

Had Savage actually taken the time to read the source document – "The Legal Status of Women Under Federal Law" – he would have seen that it was originally written in 1974 for the Columbia Law School Equal Rights Advocacy Project.[59] Ginsberg, her co-author and student researchers surveyed the United States Code for gender-specific language, examined that language and made recommendations where gender-neutral language would be more precise. For example, some older laws codified in the Code assumed that certain positions would only be filled by men and referred to, for example, "miners and their wives." Ginsberg's group sought to change that wording to reflect the reality of women in the workforce and in other segments of modern society.

Let's take Savage's claims one by one:

Lower the age of sexual consent to 12: In this section, Ginsburg's group references a bill presented to the U.S. Senate in 1973 (S-1400) by the administration of ... wait a minute ...

---

59 "Report of Columbia Law School Equal Rights Advocacy Project, The Legal Status ofWomen Under Federal Law," 1974.

Richard M. Nixon?! In that bill, the definition of rape includes the provision that the victim is less than 12 years old. Rather than lower the "age of consent," as Savage pruriently states, the bill sought to lower the age threshold of those who could be considered rape victims.

Legalize prostitution: Ginsberg's group argues that, "Prostitution, as a consensual act between adults, is arguably within the zone of privacy protected by" U.S. Supreme Court decisions based on privacy rights, such as Roe v. Wade. The group does argue that prostitution should be decriminalized.

Draft women and send them into combat: Ginsberg's group does assert that "equal rights and responsibilities for men and women implies that women must be subject to draft registration if men are." (Page 197.) That's not a surprising point of view considering the Equal Rights Amendment debates that were ongoing at the time.

The group also advocates for women in combat positions, reasoning that there should be no impediments to women working their way up the ranks in the uniformed services. As the group writes on pages 39-40 in the report, "On the other hand, eliminating sex per se as an assignment determinant will make it possible for women to advance in the military as far as their talents and aspirations permit."

Although in this book Savage seems shocked at the idea of women in combat, on his radio show Savage regularly pay homage to women fighting in Afghanistan and Iraq.

All-boy and all-girl social groups should be sexually integrated: Savage's imprecise writing – no doubt exacerbated by the fact he's quoting from someone else's work — makes it a little difficult to know about which section he's talking, so I'll deal with both of them. In the first instance, Ginsberg's group was referring to the fact that although the 4-H organization had ceased referring to itself as "4-H Boys Clubs" and "4-H Girls Clubs, "federal legislation authorizing payments to the organization did not reflect their merger. Ginsberg's group wrote that the citation in the Code should reflect the new name. They were not advocating for the "sexual integration" of all or any boys and girls clubs.

In the second instance, Ginsberg's group notes that while organizations such as Boys Clubs of America and Big Brothers existed for boys, no similar groups existed for girls. Noting the positive benefits these groups extended to their members, Ginsberg's group recommended that similar organizations – under the umbrella of a larger organization – be created for girls.

Ginsberg's group notes that federally created groups for youth – there's no mention of private groups — should be open to both girls and boys. The group's report suggests that in some cases, sexually segregated groups are appropriate, but in others, which are not named, integration may be the better routes.

"A lone ranger federal magistrate, Chief U.S. District Judge Thelton Henderson, a Jimmy

Carter appointee, heard the case and denied the wishes of nearly 5 million Californians by single-handedly overturning Prop. 209." **The Enemy Within, page 33.**

Savage is writing about the California Civil Rights Initiative, otherwise known as Proposition 209, which was passed by California voters in 1996. The measure effectively dismantled affirmative action hiring in the state. The ACLU and other groups immediately sued, claiming that Prop. 209 was unconstitutional.

Judge Henderson, of the Northern District Court of Appeals, agreed with the ACLU and stayed implementation of the measure. And as far as Savage's book is concerned (published in 2003, by the way), that's the end of the story.

But what Savage doesn't tell his readers is that by September 1997, the U.S. Supreme Court refused to hear an appeal of the 9th Circuit Court of Appeals reversal of Henderson's decision, thereby allowing California to implement Prop. 209.[60]

Now, why would Savage neglect to point out that "the wishes of nearly 5 million Californians", as he writes, was eventually upheld by the courts? Because that would kill his thesis that America's judges are running rampant, tearing up the Constitution as they go.

60　"Supreme Court refuses to block California end to set-asides," by Frank J. Murray, *The Washington Times*, Sept. 5, 1997.

"His closing comments blasted people with 'religious convictions' saying 'they are not free … to enforce their views, their religious convictions, or their philosophies on all other members of a democratic society.'" **The Enemy Within, page 34.**

Here Savage is talking about a decision rendered in March 1996 by the 9th Circuit Court of Appeals, which struck down a Washington state statute that made it a felony to help someone commit suicide. The majority opinion was written by Judge Stephen Reinhardt.

Savage selectively quoted from the judge's statement, making it seem as though Reinhardt was attacking people with firm religious beliefs. Here's what the judge *actually* wrote:

"Under our constitutional system, neither the state nor the majority of the people in a state can impose its will upon the individual in a matter so highly 'central to personal dignity and autonomy,' (Casey, 112 S. Ct. at 2807). Those who believe strongly that death must come without physician assistance are free to follow that creed, be they doctors or patients. They are not free, however, to force their views, their religious convictions, or their philosophies on all the other members of a democratic society, and to compel those whose values differ with theirs to die painful, protracted, and agonizing deaths."[61]

---

61   9th Circuit Court of Appeals, Compassion in Dying vs. State of Washington, No. 94-35534 filed May 28, 1996

How did Savage get this so wrong? The answer, as I have noted in other instances, lies in Savage's intellectual laziness.

Savage cites as his source a July 3, 2002 article written by Greg Hoadley for the Center for Reclaiming America for Christ, an offshoot of the Coral Ridge Ministries of Ft. Lauderdale, Florida. Interestingly, in his reference Savage identifies the group as simply "Center for Reclaiming America." He must have missed the "for Christ" part.

At any rate, Hoadley's article misrepresents and misquotes Reinhardt's opinion, and Savage repeats the misstatements apparently without checking the source. Sloppy research by someone else leads to diminished credibility for Savage.

Clearly, Reinhardt was not aiming his comments solely at those with "religious convictions," as Savage would have his readers believe. Rather, he directed his comments at those in the majority who would impose their will on individuals who did not share their beliefs, regardless of the method.

And Reinhardt did not write "enforce," as Savage and Hoadley misquoted. Of course, "enforce" sounds better than "force," especially when you're trying to insinuate someone's actions are inspired by religious bigotry.

Savage (and Hoadley) also asserted that Reinhardt tried to make his case by citing public opinion polls:

> *"... Reinhardt ... cited public opinion polls as a basis for overturning the will of the people."*
> **The Savage Nation, Page 33.**

What Reinhardt actually did was cite some public opinion polls on the subject of assisted suicide in a section of his opinion entitled "Current Societal Attitudes," which followed a section about historical attitudes toward suicide. There was no other mention made of the polls, except in the attempt to frame the issue in some sort of historical perspective. Reinhardt's final opinion does not mention any reliance on "public opinion," contrary to Savage's assertion.

Republicans

> *"What's most saddening about the attack on Miguel Estrada by the leftists and their cohorts in the media is this: the Republicans were all talk. Republicans failed to act on their convictions for two years …They could have played hardball with the Schumer squad. They could have forced an end to the Dems filibuster. But not one person stood up against this character assassination."*
> **The Enemy Within, page 27.**

Savage is referring to the opposition put up by Democrats to President George W. Bush's nomination of Miguel Estrada to the U.S. Court of Appeals. Savage appears to be wearing his "independent conservative" hat here. The fact is that the Senate Republicans tried time and again to break the Democrats' filibuster, but failed to get the necessary 60 votes.[62]

---

62 "Senators fail to end debate on Estrada," Fox News, March 6, 2003. http://www.foxnews.com/story/0,2933,80439,00.html

Religion, the U.S. Constitution and the Myth of Christian Nationalism

"The Founding Fathers guaranteed us 'freedom of religion' not 'freedom from religion.' ... The boll weevils on the left claim the Constitution has erected a 'wall of separation between church and state.' ... But they're wrong. The alleged 'wall of separation' doesn't exist, it cannot be found in any of the constitutional documents. Period."
The Savage Nation, page 71.

Neither can a direct reference to any god.

Nowhere in the Constitution is a god -- Christian or otherwise -- mentioned. Why is that?

Why would these God-fearing men choose to leave out any mention of the Creator in the blueprint for the new government, which is what the Constitution is?

Because while many of them were religious, most understood that the United States would be better off run by a civil government, rather than a theocracy.

Savage's definitive-sounding statements notwithstanding, there is no black and white answer on the question. The Founders were sufficiently ambiguous in their statements and writings to give advocates of either position more than enough ammunition.

For example, Savage quotes Thomas Jefferson to buttress his argument about the intent of the founders concerning religion.

But try this on for size, from a letter from Jefferson to Alexander von Humboldt in 1831:

"History I believe furnishes no example of a priest-ridden people maintaining a free civil government. This marks the lowest grade of ignorance, of which their political as well as religious leaders will always avail themselves for their own purpose."

Savage also quotes Benjamin Franklin who, in a speech given to the Constitutional Convention on Thursday, June 28, 1787, suggested that after three or four weeks of deliberations having gone nowhere, matters might be helped by a morning prayer.

> *"How did they respond? They started to pray at their meetings, a tradition the House and the Senate still embrace today."* **The Savage Nation, page 72.**

Hmm. If Savage had continued to read the document (if he

read it at all), he would have seen this note, written by Franklin:

"The Convention, except three or four persons, thought prayers unnecessary."[63]

The truth is that Jefferson and a number of his colleagues repeatedly contradicted themselves in matters of church and state.

So, it's really difficult to state unequivocally how they felt. And as far as Savage's notion that the wall between church and state is an invention of the left, consider this:

"Because Religion be exempt from the authority of the Society at large, still less can it be subject to that of the Legislative Body. The latter are but the creatures and vicegerents of the former. Their jurisdiction is both derivative and limited: it is limited with regard to the co-ordinate departments, more necessarily is it limited with regard to the constituents.

"The preservation of a free Government requires not merely, that the metes and bounds which separate each department of power be invariably maintained; but more especially that neither of them be suffered to overleap the great Barrier which defends the rights of the people. The Rulers who are guilty of such an encroachment, exceed the commission from which they derive their authority, and are Tyrants. The People who submit to it are governed by laws made neither by themselves nor by an

---

63   "Records of the Federal Convention", June 28, 1787:
     http://www.americanrhetoric.com/images/BenFranklin3.JPG

authority derived from them, and are slaves.[64]

Those were the words of James Madison, considered by historians to be the father of the U.S. Constitution.

And, finally, there's this:

"The unique thing about America is a wall in our Constitution separating church and state. It guarantees there will never be a state religion in this land, but at the same time it makes sure that every single American is free to choose and practice his or her religious beliefs or to choose no religion at all. Their rights shall not be questioned or violated by the state."[65]

Those words were spoken by none other than Ronald Reagan, the Right's poster boy. Why is it that no one ever quotes him on this subject?

"Here, then, is a 'generic' prayer delivered by President Dwight Eisenhower in his second inaugural address: 'Give us the power to discern clearly ...'" **The Savage Nation, page 77.**

I won't reproduce the entire entry because it's not germane to my comments. First, Savage got the date wrong. This snippet is from Eisenhower's *first* inaugural address[66]. Second, it is not

---

64 "Memorial and Remonstrance," James Madison:
http://candst.tripod.com/tnppage/memorial.htm
65 Ronald Reagan, remarks at the International Convention of B'nai B'rith, Sept. 6, 1984.
66 Dwight D. Eisenhower, first inaugural address, Jan. 20, 1953.
http://www.americanrhetoric.com/speeches/
dwighteisenhowerfirstinaugural.htm

generic, in that it starts with "Almighty God," although Savage left out that part, which clearly establishes adherence to a specific belief system. That, of course, would interfere with his premise, which was that this prayer was generic and, therefore, should not offend anyone.

> *"Now, who are we going to believe about Pious*
> *(sic) XII – a blathering earringed script reader*
> *on 60 Minutes, with no proof for his slanders?"*
> **The Savage Nation, page 81.**

Savage was fulminating about a 60 Minutes broadcast on March 19, 2000, in which co-host Ed Bradley (who wears an earring) reported on a book called Hitler's Pope, written by John Cornwell. Cornwell was a fellow at Jesus College, Cambridge University in England when he did his research into the activities of Pope Pius XII during World War II.

Pius had been criticized by those who thought he did not do enough to save Jews during the Holocaust. His supporters contend he did what he could and, some say, he helped save hundreds of thousands of Jews by the war's end.

The transcript[67] of the broadcast shows that Savage went a little overboard in his criticism. Bradley talks to Cornwell, who, contrary to what Savage asserts, does back up his charges, as

---

67 "Pope Pius XII: Hitler's Pope?" 60 Minutes, CBS News, March 19, 2000: http://hist.academic.claremontmckenna.edu/jpetropoulos/documents/ sixtymin.htm

well as others. Among his other interviews is a woman who was among about 1,000 Jews rounded up by Nazis and held in an old military college in Rome before being sent to a concentration camp, who condemned Pius for not risking himself and speaking out.

News programs such as 60 Minutes are ripe targets for the Right-wing, which has been blathering on for years about the "liberal media." Savage takes the obligatory shots in another attempt to rally his troops around his flag.

Now, if he really wanted to fulminate, he should have checked out the October, 2000 report issued by the International Catholic-Jewish Historical Commission,[68] which was charged by the Holy See to investigate questions of Pius' behavior during World War II.

That report raised 47 questions that needed to be answered by the submission by the Vatican of more documents. The documents were never forthcoming, and the commission later disbanded.

These questions, some of which refer to apparently unanswered pleas to the Pope to take a strong stand against what the Germans were doing to Jews, are more damning to the Pope's legacy than the 60 Minutes report.

Could that be why Savage ignored the report?

---

68 "The Vatican and the Holocaust: A Preliminary Report," International Catholic-Jewish Historical Commission, October, 2000.

*"The effects of ultraliberalism and the intoler-
ance it breeds can be increasingly found in
the churched community. Take, for example, a
pseudoreligious or semireligious day school in
Manhattan ... They banned the celebration of
Mother's Day ...Watch what happens when ...
any other private religious institution, attempts
to appease the anti-God Commu-Nazis."*
The Savage Nation, pages 84-85.

Savage is venting his spleen on the decision by the Rodeph
Sholom Day School (www.rodephshalom.org) to not have its
older students celebrate Mother's Day or Father's Day. The
school administration felt that the celebrations served no edu-
cational purpose, and that they might upset those who came
from non-traditional families, such as one-parent families.

Savage doesn't mention that, though. He'd rather his reader
believe the celebrations were cancelled because of some religious persecution. And he also makes it seem as though the ban
applied to all students, when it only applied to those older than
four years.

*"Hey Chucky, here's a tip since you obviously
misinterpreted American government in junior
high. Read the U.S. Constitution. Specifically,
Article Six, which says, '[N]o religious test shall
ever be required as a qualification to any office*

or public trust under the United States.' "
The Enemy Within, page 27.

As he does throughout his trilogy, Savage here attempts to reinforce his point by cherry-picking a segment of something that, if the entire selection were read, would actually refute his statement.

This quote, directed to U.S. Sen. Charles Schumer, a Democrat from New York, is part of a larger segment in which Savage is trying to prove that Schumer's opposition in 2001 to President Bush's nomination of Miguel Estrada to the U.S. Court of Appeals was based on religion. Savage's argument is that Schumer is opposed to Estrada simply because he is a Catholic and holds very traditional Catholic views.

By quoting Article 6 of the U.S. Constitution, Savage tries to make the point that religion cannot be used to disqualify federal office holders. But that's not what Article 6 was meant to do.

First of all, it would be helpful to see the entire article:

"All debts contracted and engagements entered into, before the adoption of this Constitution, shall be as valid against the United States under this Constitution, as under the Confederation.

"This Constitution, and the laws of the United States which shall be made in pursuance thereof; and all treaties made, or which shall be made, under the authority of the United States, shall be the supreme law of the land; and the judges in every state shall be bound thereby, anything in the Constitution or laws of any State to the contrary notwithstanding.

"The Senators and Representatives before mentioned, and the members of the several state legislatures, and all executive and judicial officers, both of the United States and of the several states, shall be bound by oath or affirmation, to support this Constitution; but no religious test shall ever be required as a qualification to any office or public trust under the United States."[69]

Article 6 was actually intended to prohibit requiring adherence to the prevailing religious belief as a prerequisite for public office. This was done to solidify the much-maligned separation of church and state in American government, a separation that even Thomas Jefferson, hardly an atheist, supported.[70]

Many state-backed religious sects were established in the American colonies which required adherence to their beliefs for basic rights and privileges, such as voting and holding elected office. In Massachusetts, for example, Quakers were *hanged* for their beliefs.

Article 6 was an attempt by the framers to inoculate the federal government against the tide of religious discrimination and intolerance rising in some of the newly formed states, where adherents to state-backed religions were denying to non-believers basic rights.

---

69   U.S. Constitution, Legal Information Institute.
     http://www.law.cornell.edu/constitution/constitution.articlevi.html
70   Thomas Jefferson letter to Danbury Baptist Association, Jan. 1, 1802.

*"Just a few short decades after the founding of
America, Daniel Webster, a real statesman and
America's foremost advocate of nationalism during his day, felt compelled to remind his contem-
poraries, 'Our ancestors established their system
of government on morality and religious sentiment. Moral habits, they believed, cannot safely
be trusted on any other foundation than religious
principle, nor any government be secure which is
not supported by moral habits.' "*
The Enemy Within, page 130.

Savage is quoting from Webster's "Plymouth Oration,"
delivered in 1820 on the anniversary of the pilgrims' landing at
Plymouth Rock. He attempts to buttress his argument that the
Founders created this country and its formative documents on
Judeo-Christian mores.

But, as usual, he leaves out the quote's context, so as not
to muddy his argument. Webster delivered that statement as
a preamble to his comments against the slave trade, which he
called a "contamination" against which "every feeling of hu-
manity must forever revolt."

Also included in that oration, which Savage ignores, is the
following: "Of our system of government the first thing to be
said is, that it is really and practically a free system. It origi-

nates entirely with the people, and rests on no other foundation than their assent."[71]

> *"The Supremes are so blind, I must remind them that the author of the First Amendment, James Madison, argued vigorously on behalf of the (Ten) Commandments. Madison said, 'We have staked the whole future of all our political institu-tions ... upon the capacity of each and all of us to govern ourselves, to sustain ourselves, according to the Ten Commandments of God.' "*
>
> **The Enemy Within, page 140.**

Savage cites as his source for the quote *America's God and Country Encyclopedia of Quotations* by William J. Federer. This quote is generally referenced to another Christian Nationalist, David Barton.

Savage apparently did not conduct any primary research on the subject. If he had, he would have discovered that the quote, if not completely a fabrication, is highly questioned by historians.

The quote, for which no direct attribution to Madison has been found, has been debunked since at least the mid-1990s.[72]

In a 1993 letter on the subject, David Mattern, one of the editors of The Madison Papers, writes to a correspondent that

---

71   www.gutenberg.org/dirs/etext05/8sweb10h.htm#03
72   http://www.blogsforbush.com/mt/archives/007248.html

he and his partner "did not find anything in our files remotely like the sentiment expressed in the extract you sent us. In addition, the idea is inconsistent with everything we know about Madison's views on religion and government, views which he expressed time and time again in public and in private."

Views such as this one, expressed in a July 10, 1822 letter to Edward Livingston, (which can be found at candst.tripod.com/tnppage/qmadison.htm): "Every new and successful example, therefore, of a perfect separation between the ecclesiastical and civil matters, is of importance; and I have no doubt that every new example will succeed, as every past one has done, in showing that religion and Government will both exist in greater purity the less they are mixed together."

Or Madison's interpretation of the First Amendment: "Congress should not establish a religion and enforce the legal observation of it by law, nor compel men to worship God in any manner contrary to their conscience, or that one sect might obtain a pre-eminence, or two combined together, and establish a religion to which they would compel others to conform."

> *"While it is true that some of the better principles of our Constitution and Bill of Rights are derived directly from the Bible ..."* **Liberalism is a Mental Disorder, page XV.**

This is yet another time when Savage makes a blanket assertion with no backup. Which of those principles are the "better" ones, anyway? In fact, nowhere in the Constitution[73] or the amendments that comprise the Bill of Rights[74] is there any mention of religion or any god. Both documents are essentially blueprints for civil government, pretty cut and dried as those things go. No overarching, grandiose statements about the Divinity (or Providence, as they termed it in those days), no pledge of allegiance or submission to any religion's god.

Right-wing propagandists such as Savage like to peddle the myth that both documents are Bible-based, which fits in nicely with their view that the country's laws should be based on Biblical principles.

Well, here's a Biblical principle taken right from Proverbs 18:6 (Amplified Bible): "A (self-confident) fool's lips bring contention and his mouth invites a beating."

73 The United States' Constitution:
    http://www.house.gov/Constitution/Constitution.html
74 Bill of Rights:
    http://www.house.gov/Constitution/Amend.html

Universal Health Insurance

"The next time a Democrat proposes an expansion of government-funded health insurance for all lower and middle income families … think Dead Man's Pants." **The Enemy Within, page 9.**

Savage tries to weave some social commentary into a story about his father regularly bringing him pants that he had bought at estate sales. Whatever. In this quote, Savage is referring to the Children's Health Insurance Program, which served more than 2.5 million children whose families earned too much to qualify for Medicaid but could not afford their own insurance. (The reader wouldn't know this unless he checked the endnote.)

Hillary Clinton, as a candidate for U.S. Senate, suggested raising the income eligibility limit for a *family of four* from $31,000 to $51,000 a year. She also suggested making subsidized health care available to adults who earn less than 300 percent of the federal poverty level.

But had Savage included that tidbit he may not have been

able to elicit the response for which he was looking, which was outrage at the thought of a blanket increase in what many Conservatives feel is a handout. After all, who can say they'd deny health care for children?

Indeed.

> *"When Tom Daschle blasts a tax cut as a means to boost the economy while proposing to provide non-working persons health-care benefits ... think Dead Man's Pants."* **The Enemy Within, page 9.**

Savage cites a Jan. 4, 2002 CNN.com story about then-Senate Majority Leader Tom Daschle's comments about Bush's economic stimulus plan at the Center for National Policy, a Washington, D.C.-based think tank.

The phrase "non-working persons" is Savage's way of trying to obfuscate what Daschle actually said and present it in as negative a way as possible. Daschle's actual comment, according to CNN was that "any stimulus package ... should include health care benefits for workers who lost their jobs."[75]

The reality – that Daschle is trying to look out for people who lost their jobs – is a little different from the picture Savage paints, which is that Daschle just wants to extend health benefits to anyone who isn't working.

---

75 "Daschle criticizes Bush tax cut, offers economic boost plan," Jan. 4, 2002, CNN.com. http://archives.cnn.com/2002/ALLPOLITICS/01/04/daschle.economy/index.html

"Never mind the fact socialized medicine is a flop. Everywhere it's been tried, it's been a complete failure. It's Third World medicine. Hear me. This neo-Marxist practice is the surest way to bankrupt the economy and destroy America." **The Enemy Within, page 51.**

Savage is fond of making grandiose statements without backing them up with the facts. There is ample evidence that universal health care – which the Right-wingers call socialized medicine – actually is working in places such as Canada. And by what benchmark do I say that? Canadians have longer life spans than Americans and a lower infant mortality rate. Plus, Canada spends about 10 percent of its gross domestic product to provide health care to all its citizens. By contrast, health care costs eat up about 14 percent of the US's gross domestic product, even though 45 million Americans have no health insurance.[76]

So which system is failing, endangering the country's economy?

"For years, we've heard Hillary, Gephardt, Daschle, Lieberman and Gore prescribing free drugs." **The Enemy Within, page 51.**

Well, not really. Let's take the prescription drug plan espoused by Al Gore during his 2000 run for the presidency.

---

76 "In Critical Condition: Health Care in America," by Barry Brown, the *San Francisco Chronicle*, Oct. 14, 2004.

What Gore proposed was a plan through which Medicare would pay half the cost of prescriptions for most, and the entire cost for those who are poor or who have large medical expenses.[77] That's similar to a plan that President Bill Clinton supported in 1999, with the help of then-House Minority leader Dick Gephardt. In fact, during the 2004 presidential campaign, the Democrats advocated for a similar plan by which most beneficiaries would pay part of the cost. There was no wholesale giving away of prescriptions, as Savage alleges.

> *"These are the facts. While there was universal health-care in Russia, it was a poor system for the average Soviet citizen."* **The Enemy Within, page 52.**

So let me get this straight. With all the other examples around (Canada, Great Britain, the Netherlands), Savage chooses to use the Russian model? Why bother to mention that the Soviet system was rife with corruption, which *might* have had a negative effect on how it was delivered?

Are there problems with universal health care in the countries that have adopted it? Sure. No system is perfect. But Savage goes on page after page in *The Enemy Within* giving mostly his opinion on the evils of health care for all, while providing just a few instances where there have been problems. Along the

---

77   "Al Gore on Medicare and Medicaid," On the Issues.
       http://www.ontheissues.org/Celeb/Al_Gore_Health_Care.htm#General

way, he makes statements such as, universal health care leads to Third-World medicine, or universal health care will bankrupt the nation.

But Savage does give us an idea of what is truly behind his hatred of universal health care on page 52:

> *"Universal health care is a carrion call for the bottom feeders out there who think I owe them a living. They think I owe them health-care, housing, a car, a chicken in every pot and pot for every chicken! What gives them the right to reach into my pocket for a handout?"*

And on page 54, Savage rails against Canada's system, alleging that access to health care is "largely unavailable."

> *"With an extreme shortage of doctors, nurses and hospital beds, the wait for basic treatment is horrendous."*

Again, Savage provides no backup for this wild claim. And, if this assertion is true, how does Savage explain the relatively high life span of Canadians versus Americans?

> *"I knew it wasn't a big issue in America. I knew most Americans, while somewhat concerned, did not put it as a top priority. And yet the out-of touch Democrats kept harping on this. Post election analysis revealed just 8 percent of voters*

*considered health care when placing their vote.
Just 8 percent!"* **Liberalism is a Mental
Disorder, page XXII.**

Although he doesn't mention it, Savage is probably referring to a CNN Exit Poll conducted during the 2004 presidential
election between George Bush and John Kerry. In that poll, 8
percent of respondents listed health care as their primary issue,
behind moral values, economy, terrorism and Iraq. Still, Savage
fails to mention that 93 percent of those respondents said they
were "somewhat" or "very" concerned about the cost of health
care.[78] Now why leave that out?

Also, a Harris Interactive poll conducted between Oct. 20
and 25, 2004, for the Wall Street Journal showed that 42 percent of the respondents said there are health care issues that
may influence the way they vote, and that 24 percent of those
said the total cost of health care is their main issue.[79]

Further, the poll showed that respondents felt John Kerry
would do a better job of addressing health care issues than
George W. Bush by a margin of 45 percent to 36 percent.[80]

So it seems that Americans are much more concerned about
health care and its costs than Savage would have us believe.

---

78 CNN.com Exit poll, http://www.cnn.com/ELECTION/2004/pages/
    results/states/US/P/00/epolls.0.html.
79 Harris Interactive Poll: http://www.harrisinteractive.com/news/news-
    letters/wsjhealthnews/WSJOnline_HI_Health-CarePoll2004vol3_
    iss21.pdf.
80 Ibid

Immigrants, legal and otherwise

"(T)he liberal socialists, who believe in open borders, are pressuring the Immigration and Naturalization Service to place water stations in the desert." **The Enemy Within, page 6.**

Savage is harping here on one of his constant themes, the Liberal "indifference" to the "flood" of illegal immigrants into this country. He cites as his reference an editorial that ran in the July 2, 2001 issue of the Wall Street Journal, written by its editor, Robert L. Bartley.[81] So, to Savage, the Wall Street Journal is a "liberal socialist" publication. And there's no reference in Bartley's editorial to placing water stations in the desert, so we don't know where that came from. But in *Liberalism is a Mental Disorder*, what does that matter?

---

81 "Open NAFTA Borders?Why Not?" By Robert L. Bartley, *The Wall Street Journal*, July 2, 2001. http://www.opinionjournal.com/columnists/ rbartley/?id=95000738

But there's another subtle point here. Savage cites the Bartley editorial after he states his opinion that government leaders are doing nothing about illegal immigration, "even in the wake of 9/11," although the editorial ran two months before the terrorist attacks of Sept. 11, 2001.

In writing about Arizona's Proposition 200, which requires proof of citizenship to vote, denies monetary benefits to illegal aliens and requires public employees to report violations, Savage opined:

> *"The reaction south of the border was criminal and terroristic! Who gave Mexico the right to dictate American policy?"* **Liberalism is a Mental Disorder, page XII.**

Calling Mexico's reaction "criminal and terroristic" is a bit over the top, but par for the course for Savage. Mexican officials said they would help the Mexican American Legal Defense and Education Fund (MALDEF) fight the proposition, and, if that didn't work, perhaps take the matter to an international tribunal such as the United Nations.

Critics said that Arizona's Proposition 200 took things a little too far. Among its deficiencies, they said, was that its vague prohibition on public services would make it difficult to enforce. And it didn't even deal with the underlying problem, our broken immigration system.

As it turned out, a lawsuit filed by MALDEF was dismissed

in August, 2005, by a three-judge Court of Appeals panel. The judges ruled that the plaintiffs had failed to show they were harmed by the measure.

> *"As I was working on this book, I came across an article that sickened me. It's the story of Richard Gonzales, Louis Gomez and Carlos Reyna, three U.S. Immigration officers who had made thousands of arrests without prior incident. These hard-working, uncorruptable (sic) men were fined and sent to jail. Their crime? They failed to give timely medical treatment to an illegal alien who had been injured during a raid."*
>
> **Liberalism is a Mental Disorder, page 59.**

Well, it's not quite as simple as Savage would have us believe.

The three INS agents were convicted in connection with the death of Serafin Olvera-Carrera following a 2001 raid on a home in a Houston, Texas suburb. The injury to which Savage alludes was actually a severe beating given to Olvera-Carrera, to the point where he was paralyzed. According to the U.S. Attorney for the southern district of Texas, Olvera-Carrera asked for help several times, but was ignored. The government also alleged that Gonzales sprayed him in the face with pepper spray "to see if he would budge."

Medical care was not provided to Olvera-Carrera for seven hours. The INS agents said they thought he was faking.

Olvera-Carrera died 11 months after the incident. A 15-month investigation was followed by a four-week trial in which the three were found guilty.[82]

His family was later awarded $2.15 million by a federal judge.

Writing about the porous border with Mexico, and its effect on border county hospitals:

> *"In 2000, San Diego's Scripps Memorial Hospital was forced to close because it was losing $5 million a year, mostly due to having to provide care to illegal aliens that was not reimbursed. "Complicating the picture is the exodus of doctors. Border-area hospitals report that they are short physicians and surgeons because these skilled professionals left for positions where their salaries are not tied to a mass of illegal aliens who skip out on their bills."* **Liberalism is a Mental Disorder, page 70.**

Savage is quoting an article entitled, "Border Hospitals on the Brink," from the June 21, 2000 issue of the left-leaning *Mother Jones Magazine*.

How nice for Mother Jones.

Savage omits some of the facts that were included in the

---

82 "INS officers to serve prison terms for violating the civil rights of Serafin Olvera Carrera," U.S. Department of Justice press release, Feb. 2, 2004.

article, choosing to let his readers assume that the hospitals' problems are caused by the normal influx of illegal immigrants. Many times the illegals did leave without paying, and the federal government did not make up the shortfall. But what Savage doesn't say is that, according to the article, one reason for the increase in illegals having to go to the hospital is that an INS crackdown on main points of entry has forced them to adapt and move to crossing points in more rugged country.[83]

As a result, people who succumbed to ailments such as heat stroke were clogging the emergency rooms of nearby hospitals, which were bound by law to treat them.

> *"Here's another shocker: In early October 2004, Health and Human Services Secretary Tommy Thompson announced that American tax dollars were being spent in Mexico in medical clinics. For what? To provide Mexicans prenatal care! At least Thompson, while making the announcement, was honest enough to say, 'Well, we're doing this because if we can prevent illness down there they won't bring it here."* **Liberalism is a Mental Disorder, page 70.**

Savage completely misquotes this news nugget from Tucson, Arizona's KOLD TV. Had he actually read the story, his *own*

---

83 "Border Hospitals on the Brink," MotherJones.com. June 21, 2000
    http://www.motherjones.com/news/feature/2000/06/
    border_hospitals.html

citation, by the way, he would have discovered that the US was donating more than $1 million for a CT scanner to help a general hospital in Nogales, Sonora treat patients with head trauma and to build two new operating rooms.[84]

There was no mention anywhere in the story of "prenatal care," as Savage asserts. Also missing is the quote Savage attributes to Thompson, the one about preventing illness down there so they won't bring it here.

What Thompson actually said, according to the piece cited by Savage, was, "What we're doing is reaching out and you got to realize disease knows no borders."

Sure, the sentiment may have been the same, but here's my point. Any first year college student who finished a basic journalism course knows that anything that appears in between quotes is sacred, it does not get altered. Apparently, Savage skipped that course. Sort of odd, considering he once applied to be the dean of U.C. Berkeley's School of Journalism. (He didn't even get called for an interview and later sued for discrimination, based on his contention that he was overlooked because he is a white man. Of course, the fact that he had no journalism experience and had been on the radio only several years at the time played no role in the school's decision.)

---

84 "American Taxpayers Funding Health Care in Mexico, http://www.kold.com/global//story.asp?s=2416643

"(U.S. Immigration and Customs Enforcement) prevented the migration of 150 Lilac Crowned and Mexican Redhead Amazon parrots. A spokesperson from WildAid, whose name isn't important, said, 'The illegal bird trade causes the death of hundreds of thousands of birds, threatens some with extinction, and poses a serious risk of disease ...'

"Let's stop right there. Last time I checked we were at war with Islamofascism, not the parrot kingdom. And these bird brains are worried about the potential deaths of smuggled birds? ... We don't have enough border guards to prevent the flood of illegal aliens from swamping our shores, but we're supposed to stop the flow of illegal parrots?" **Liberalism is a Mental Disorder, pages 78-79.**

I guess Savage just can't resist an opportunity for glibness. The birds referenced in that release (which you can read for yourself at www.wildaid.org/index.asp?CID=8&PID=66&SUBID=&TERID=93) weren't "migrating," they were being illegally smuggled across the border. And why is that important? Ever hear of avian flu? Had Savage been intellectually honest and finished the first quote, his readers would have read WildAid executive director Peter Knights (something more than a spokesperson) point that out. Here's the entire quote: "The illegal bird trade causes the death of hundreds of thousands of birds, threatens some with extinction and poses a serious risk of disease to US agriculture to human health (e.g. Avian Influenza)."

Savage omits mention of what could be a scourge for American farmers, but, ironically, later in the book while talking about the lifting of a 90-year-old ban on Mexican avocados and the disastrous effect it would have on California avocado growers, Savage asks rhetorically, "What can be more sacred than the family farm?"

So what is it, Savage? Short attention span or do you just not pay attention to what you write?

Savage goes on in *Liberalism* to write about the campaign by People for the Ethical Treatment of Animals to convince people to stop eating fish. The reason, PETA claims, is that fish have feelings too, and we shouldn't be sticking hooks in their lips and hauling them out of the sea.

To back up his contention, Savage on page 97 quotes Benjamin Franklin when he writes about how he decided to once again eat "flesh" after being a vegetarian. Franklin recalled how friends had caught and cooked some fish, which began smelling very good to him. Searching for a reason to join in their meal, Franklin remembered that he had seen smaller fish taken out of the stomachs of larger fish when the latter were cut open.

"Then, thought I, if you eat one another, I don't see why we mayn't eat you," Savage quotes Franklin as writing. Savage ends his quote there. The next sentence, however, might have weakened his argument: "So convenient a thing it is to be a reasonable Creature, since it enables one to find or make a Reason for every thing one has a mind to do." (You can read about the incident here: www.earlyamerica.com/lives/franklin/chapt4/index.html).

> *"Using the latest available figures, the total prison population as of December 2002 was 2,166,260 inmates. Of that, 29 percent are illegal aliens -- or, put another way, more than three in ten of the prisoners incarcerated don't even belong in our country."* **Liberalism is a Mental Disorder, page 83.**

This is one of Savage's favorite statistics. He cites as his source a press release from the U.S. Department of Justice that was issued in 2003.

Reading that release, it's difficult if not impossible to see where Savage came up with his three in ten figure. It's just not there. What's not hard to see, though, is the DOJ's reporting that in 2002 (the latest year cited in a report located at www.ojp.usdoj.gov/bjs/pub /pdf/p02.pdf) there were a total of 21,065 people being held by the U.S. Bureau of Immigration and Customs Enforcement for immigration violations. That number was split among federal jails, local jails and jails run by or for the BICE. I'm no math whiz, but even I know that 21,065 is nowhere near 29 percent of 2.2 million.

Liberals and the (Liberal) Media

"Anyone in the media who does not refer to Rat Boy as a traitor is a distorter of the facts and a propagandist for him." **The Savage Nation, page 45.**

Actually, anyone in the media who doesn't refer to John Walker Lindh – also known as the "American Taliban" and, as Savage likes to say, "Ratboy" – as a traitor is being a responsible journalist.

Lindh, you will remember, is the California man who was captured in 2001 by the Northern Alliance and then turned over to the United States for questioning. Eventually, faced with 10 charges, Lindh plea bargained that down to two: serving in the Taliban army and carrying weapons.

For the media to call Lindh a traitor, he would have to have been convicted of treason, which he was not. Doing so anyway would open up the media outlet to a potential libel suit, something those in the corporate boardrooms tend to frown upon.

Savage is being disingenuous when he says the media which do not label Lindh a traitor are acting as his propagandist. Surely a man who once aspired to be the head of a university journalism department knows the basics of communication law?

One of Savage's favorite targets in *The Savage Nation*, as well as the other two books that comprise the trilogy, is the Cable News Network. Savage alternately refers to it as the Taliban News Network (mostly during the Afghan portion of the war against terror) and the Crescent News Network, ridicule being one of Savage's favorite weapons.

On page 46, Savage purports to paraphrase a conversation between CNN's Wolf Blitzer and Nic Robertson (whose first name he misspells) on the morale of the Taliban fighters about five weeks after the start of the Afghan war. Savage is incensed that CNN would broadcast an interview in which Robertson allegedly says that the morale of the Taliban is strong. He then "paraphrases" an interview with a Taliban fighter thusly:

"We kill America. We kill you. You can't hurt us, come on over. Death to the infidels."

The closest transcript I could find to this recollection was from a Nov. 4, 2001 broadcast[85] in which CNN's Martin Savage (ironic, huh?) interviews Robertson and asks him about Taliban

---

85 CNN transcript: "Nic Robertson: Taliban digging in for long haul." http://archives.cnn.com/2001/WORLD/asiapcf/central/11/04/ret. robertson.otsc/index.html

morale. With the bombing raids having started in early October, this would fall into Savage's time line.

It also seems to irritate Savage that Robertson was granted access to the Taliban fighters, although he could not go into military facilities. Savage said Robertson "is a British snit who looks like a towel boy in a bathhouse." (Page 46.)

Had Savage read the actual transcript rather than depend on his memory, he would have discovered what Robertson really said:

> *"From what we could see in Kandahar, which is where we've just been — and one remembers that Kandahar is really the spiritual stronghold of the Taliban, and one would expect spirits there to be better than anywhere else in the country — what we can see from the Taliban fighters we mixed with and talked to quite freely was quite a high sense of morale. They certainly don't exhibit any fear at this time. In fact, quite the opposite."*

As is his style, Savage then frames his argument in the context of World War II, another of his favorite techniques, and superimposes a CNN camera crew on board a landing craft in enemy territory. And, of course, the reporter is blabbering about how strong the enemy looks.

This is, of course, designed to anger the reader and thus convert him to Savage's belief that one cannot trust news outlets such as CNN. Better that they dial their Internet browser to michaelsavage.com to get their news.

Savage takes several pages to document how CNN is "hampering" the American war effort, all of which he backs up with examples that have no footnotes and, therefore, cannot be checked. But that doesn't matter to this propagandist, so long as he gets his audience frothing.

And he's heavy on the insults, referring at one point to CNN reporter Ashley Banfield as "the mind-slut with a big pair of glasses that they sent to Afghanistan." (Page 48).

He ends this diatribe by saying President Bush should block CNN's signal "until they stop reporting on the exact departure and arrival of our planes." (Page 49.)

> *"A Filipino immigrant went berserk in the San Francisco Bay area. He took out his handgun and shot two of his neighbors. The motive? The media blamed his depressed state of mind ... But, because he was a 'person of color,' they didn't emphasize the gun or his race, as they would have if the shooter had blue eyes and blond hair."*
> **The Savage Nation, pages 171-172.**

The *San Francisco Chronicle* stories on the shooting clearly stated that the assailant was a Filipino, and that he used a handgun.[86] I suppose the paper showed its "bias" because the

---

86 " 4 Shot to Death, Toddler Wounded in S.F. Rampage," by Janine DeFao, Ken Hoover and Steve Rubenstein, *San Francisco Chronicle*, Oct. 11, 1999.

headline didn't scream "Filipino."

Beyond that, Savage got the number of victims wrong, and neglected to mention the shooter killed himself.

> *"Another case in point about media manipulation: At the stroke of midnight on a Saturday night, California Governor 'Red' Davis passed a heroin-needle exchange bill, bowing to pressure from the radical homosexual lobby. When Monday morning rolled around, you'd never know what really took place. The newspapers reported that Davis passed a touchy-feely nurses bill, completely ignoring the needle exchange."* **The Savage Nation, page 172.**

Perhaps that's because the story about the needle exchange appeared in *Sunday's* papers.

The Sunday, Oct. 10, 1999 edition of the *San Francisco Chronicle*[87] reported on Davis signing the bill into law (governors sign bills, they don't "pass" them. Perhaps Savage needs a civics lesson.) The bill he signed, however, was a watered-down version of what needle-exchange advocates had hoped for.

Rather than allow any town to run needle exchange programs, the bill Davis signed exempted cities such as San Francisco from prosecution if its employees distributed needles.

---

87 `"Davis OKs Watered-Down Needle Law," byRobert Salladay, *San Francisco Chronicle*, Oct. 10, 1999.

Hardly the wide-ranging measure Savage would have his readers believe it was.

> *"Members of the ultra-left-wing activist organization, MoveOn, are now planted in the newsrooms of ABC, NBC, MSNBC, CNN and CNBC to manipulate news coverage."* **The Enemy Within, page 6.**

Savage cites as his reference for this "fact" a short piece that appears in the March 24, 2003 edition of American Spectator Online, the rightist publication edited by renowned crank R. Emmett Tyrell Jr. In the section called "Washington Prowler," the author quotes an unnamed MoveOn organizer who was overheard "bragging" at a bar that "they have members working in the newsrooms at CNN, ABC News and NBC ..."

No names, no further attribution, just the someone supposedly yapping at a bar to ... who? A girl he was trying to impress? A boy she was trying to impress? The point is, the Spectator published something that probably wouldn't have made it to a real newspaper's gossip page, and Savage swallowed it as gospel, simply because of where he read it, and regurgitated it to his readers without checking into its veracity himself.

> *"Take a 'scholar' at Poynter Institute who works to indoctrinate the next generation of journalists. He saw Bush's win as 'a first step toward*

the theocratic fanaticism that has poisoned the Islamic cultures around the world.' Does he actually believe President Bush will invoke the powers of his office to proclaim a jihad?" **Liberalism is a Mental Disorder, page 192.**

To back up his snarky comment, Savage cites an article from the January, 2005 issue of Citizen magazine. Unfortunately for Savage and the article's authors, Tom Hess and Karla Dial, that scholar – Roy Peter Clark – is badly misquoted.

Clark wrote an opinion column on the Poynter Web site on Nov. 4, 2004 entitled, "Confessions of an Alienated Journalist," in which he asserts that many journalists do not adequately cover the kinds of Americans who voted for Bush in 2004.

In talking about himself, Clark writes, "I attend Catholic Mass most Sundays, but in my life as a citizen I am a thorough secularist. In fact, I believe that excessive public piety is a danger to democracy, a first step toward the theocratic fanaticism that has poisoned the Islamic cultures around the world."[88]

Nothing in that quote links Bush's win to "theocratic fanaticism."

In fact, there's no evidence anywhere in the piece backing up Savage's charge. Clearly, he was too lazy to actually check the quote for himself before including it in his book, instead relying on the "research" of two writers who didn't get it right, either.

---

88 Roy Peter Clark, "Confessions of an Alienated Journalist," Poynter Online: http://www.poynter.org/content/content_view.asp?id=73946

Science and Scientists

"On February 4, 2002, the American Academy of Pediatrics released a statement – based completely on junk science, I might add – that claimed gay couples can raise children as effectively as can a traditional family. It had no genuine data to back up the claim." **The Savage Nation, page 96.**

Well, perhaps Savage only read the press release that was distributed on Feb. 4, 2002, without actually reading the technical statement the academy published. The statement includes 25 references to published studies – which, as I imagine even Savage would admit, are the ones that count – supporting the contention that children can be raised as well by a gay couple as they can by a heterosexual couple. Among the journals cited are the *American Journal of Orthopsychiatry*, *Developmental Psychology*, and the *Journal of Child Psychology and Psychiatry*. There are also several gay-oriented psychological journals, which, no doubt, led Savage to make his "junk science" claim.

But it's much easier for Savage to pander to his target reader's built-in distaste for gay lifestyles and use that to add to his bandwagon than actually read reports that might refute his argument.

> *"Al (Gore) says there's a giant hole in the ozone layer. The press take it as gospel ... Not so fast. A handful of scientists started to dig around for the truth. Guess what they found: Al's head is lost somewhere on Cloud Nine. The guy's a complete dreamer... According to scientists from Tokyo University, the ozone hole should mend completely by the year 2040 ... No more hole, except in Al's theory."* **The Savage Nation, page 198.**

Well, not so fast. Savage is so anxious to show his Republican-soldier chops and curry favor with what he hopes (at the time the book was published) will be a second George W. Bush presidency that he (as usual) neglects to truth-check his statement.

Had he checked a June 5, 2002 release prepared by the Environment News Service, Savage would have learned that the theory espoused by the Japanese scientists was challenged by a study done at NASA.

According to that release, NASA's Drew Shindell, an atmospheric scientist from the Goddard Institute for Space Studies, "used computer simulations to show that as CFCs (Chlorofluorocarbons, which are nontoxic, nonflammable chemicals containing atoms of carbon, chlorine, and fluorine that have been shown to destroy ozone in the Earth's stratosphere) decline, the ozone layer could make close to a full recovery by 2040, if global warming is not taken into account. But when CFCs, water vapor and temperature changes were combined in a computer model, ozone levels recover only slightly from their current low point by 2040.

"These computer simulations suggest that climate change from greenhouse gases may slow any anticipated ozone recovery," Shindell said. The effects of climate change need to be better accounted for as the success of international agreements, like the 1987 Montreal Protocol that banned CFCs, is tracked, he added."[89]

Savage's hysteria over Gore's advocacy of good environmental stewardship apparently has to do with his fears that, a President Gore would "slap us with regulations to minimize future damage to the ozone." (Page 199). Horrors!

> *"Leading psychiatric groups such as the American Psychiatric Association are contemplating the normalization of pedophilia – sex with children."* **The Enemy Within, page 6.**

89　"Climate Change Depletes Ozone Layer," Environment News Service, June 5, 2002. http://www.ens-newswire.com/ens/jun2002/2002-06-05-09.asp#anchor3

It's true that there was the suggestion at the APA symposium held in May 2003 to remove pedophilia from the psychiatrist's Bible, the *Diagnostic and Statistical Manual of Mental Disorders.*

But if Savage was being truly intellectually honest, he would have noted that that suggestion was never adopted. In fact, as was reported by the *Washington Times*, certainly no left-wing publication, "According to Dr. Darrel A. Reiger, APA director of research, 'The APA never had any intention of removing pedophilia from its Diagnostic and Statistical Manual of Mental Disorders. In fact, when revising the 2000 manual, the APA strengthened the criteria for pedophilia to include any action that involved molestation toward a child, regardless of whether or not the person was conflicted about it.' "[90]

---

90 "The APA Gets It Right," *The Washington Times*, June 18, 2003.
http://www.washtimes.com/op-ed/20030618-102516-7708r.htm

Afterword

I said at the outset that, for the purposes of this book, I have no real interest in Michael "Savage" Weiner's opinions. What concerned me was the at-time blatant misrepresentation of facts and the outright lying that he employs in each of the three "political trilogy" books to support those opinions.

The purpose of this book was to shine a bright light on those instances and show them for what they are.

All of us shade the truth (or even tell whoppers) at times; it's human nature. But Savage doesn't just shade the truth, he attempts to turn black into white and white into black. Fortunately, for reasonable people, he usually fails at it.

This book is not going to dissuade those who have taken up residence in the Savage Nation. Those folks who have bought into his lies will dismiss this as just more Liberal bellyaching. To which I would respond, enjoy your fantasy.

The people I am trying to reach are those who have had to

endure the constant barrage of lies, misrepresentations, hate and fear-mongering unleashed not only by Savage, but also his cohorts on the Right. The facts I have presented are backed up by citations to refute what passes for truth in Savage's books. Just because he says something is so, does not make it so.

What he also does is exploit fear and convert it to the easier-managed emotions of anger and fury. Stir in a little racism, a little blame, and you have your holocaust. How strange, the villains he disdains, he patterns.

I don't envision this book having any material affect on Savage's ratings, nor will it cost his radio show any advertisers. Madison Avenue doesn't care more about ideology than getting its message to potential customers. And with 8 million or so radio listeners, Savage does that.

I write this with a much smaller purpose in mind, to serve as another arrow in the quivers of those among us who choose to fight the good fight, to counter falsehoods with facts and to rip the cloak off the mean-spiritedness and dishonesty that so characterizes the Radical Right.

Keep the faith.

www.ingramcontent.com/pod-product-compliance
Lightning Source LLC
Chambersburg PA
CBHW051449250726
48655CB00001B/312